Praise for *Logging Off*

'Not everyone could turn a horrific family tragedy into a smart, compulsive and urgent read about the dangers of social media, but this is exactly what Adele Walton has achieved with her much-needed book *Logging Off*. She blends together scientific and social research with personal experience to bring to life the impact social media has on all our lives. As the first generation to grow up with social media throughout their childhoods, we urgently need to listen to voices like Adele's if we are to tackle the harms of this technology, while also recognising the joys and connections the internet can bring'

Sian Norris, author of *Bodies Under Siege*

'*Logging Off* is a deeply moving and powerfully argued exposé of the technologies that have come to dominate our lives. Walton masterfully demonstrates that these technologies are not neutral – they are designed to enrich their owners and harm their users. You won't look at your screens in the same way after reading this book'

Grace Blakeley, author of *Vulture Capitalism*

'*Logging Off* is a life-saving book. It's an essential deep-dive into the digital world that everyone needs to read. An important, fascinating, heart-filled page-turner of a debut'

Mikaela Loach, author of *It's Not That Radical*

'A harrowing but important read from a member of the rising generation of young people who've experienced first-hand the dangers of out-of-control tech companies and killer algorithms'

Carole Cadwalladr, *Guardian*

'*Logging Off* is a necessary and urgent account of the human cost of social media. Adele does an extraordinary job of helping understand the preventable harm that young people are experiencing. If you are a parent, lawmaker, or work in social media, *Logging Off* is a must read'

Arturo Bejar, Meta whistleblower

'*Logging Off* is a refreshing wake up to reclaim the beauty of life and authenticity of human connection. While social media has a powerful influence on our relationships and how we see the world, Adele Zeynep Walton successfully argues that we need to reassert our own agency over technology. This book is a much-needed clarion call to see the humanity in others, imbue our actions with empathy, and know when to log off so we can turn on a fulfilling life'

David Ryan Polgar, Founder and President of All Tech Is Human

'Motivated by the most tragic of circumstances, Adele Zeynep Walton combines a compendium of contemporary horror stories with a breadth of well-referenced expert testimony, to produce a vital commentary for anyone wanting to better understand our dangerous digital world. *Logging Off* offers a thought-provoking digital stocktake, a must read for concerned parents and for all who want to more safely navigate the technological perils we all face today'

Ian Russell MBE, Chair of the Molly Rose Foundation

'*Logging Off* is a vital wake-up call. In her deeply personal narrative, Adele Zeynep Walton explores how Big Tech profits from addiction, exploits our data and puts vulnerable people at risk, all while evading accountability and gaslighting us into believing this is simply what we all want. An urgent call to action for reclaiming our digital lives is now'

Daisy Greenwell, Cofounder/director, Smartphone Free Childhood

'Poignant, timely and astute, *Logging Off* is a compelling examination of how our lives have been shaped – and irrevocably changed – by the rise of digital technologies. Adele has written a must-read book on the complexities and real world costs of this new normal, and it is one that should be stocked in every single school library'

Yomi Adegoke, author of *The List*

'An equally enraging and empowering book by a fiercely talented writer and campaigner. Adele's incisive power in her observations is emboldening; her personal experiences a sobering reminder of the human cost of the unchecked Big Tech monopoly over our lives. You will leave this book ready to join the fight against online harms'

Elena Michael, Director of Not Your Porn

'Compelling and investigative, Adele Walton is the voice of Gen Z on tech. *Logging Off* holds us to account for the ills of unbounded technology, showing its unacceptable human cost and pointing towards vital solutions'

Emily Kenway, author of *The Truth About Modern Slavery*

Logging Off

The Human Cost of Our Digital World

ADELE ZEYNEP WALTON

First published in Great Britain in 2025 by Trapeze,
an imprint of The Orion Publishing Group Ltd
Carmelite House, 50 Victoria Embankment
London EC4Y 0DZ

An Hachette UK Company

The authorised representative in the EEA is Hachette Ireland, 8
Castlecourt Centre, Dublin 15, D15 XTP3, Ireland (email: info@hbgi.ie)

SRD

A CIP catalogue record for this book is
available from the British Library.

ISBN (Hardback) 978 1 3987 2292 7
ISBN (Export Trade Paperback) 978 1 3987 2772 4
ISBN (Ebook) 978 1 3987 2295 8
ISBN (Audio) 978 1 3987 2296 5

Typeset by Born Group
Printed and bound in India by Manipal Technologies Limited, Manipal

MIX
Paper | Supporting
responsible forestry
FSC
www.fsc.org
FSC™ C104740

www.orionbooks.co.uk

For Aimee x

'Grief is the way to transformation'

Dr Yuria Celidwen

Contents

INTRODUCTION

Welcome to the New World

'There is a sort of poverty of the spirit which stands in glaring contrast to our scientific and technological abundance.'

Martin Luther King Jr[1]

Technology is not neutral. As you scroll through your phone, soaking in content online, you may see something that upsets, irritates or angers you, or it could be something more extreme, something that rocks you to your core. This sparking of emotion reveals in its own small way how what we consume online can have an impact that transcends the four corners of a screen. It is an example of how the digital world is not some technological utopia but instead a warped distortion of our offline world, one that intensifies its pitfalls and maximises its risks. We are all aware that our offline world is tough, it's imperfect, harsh and, at times, traumatic. Many of us turn to our digital spaces to escape this reality. But that online haven is a fallacy and an illusion. We have created technological tools that magnify the injustices in our material world, build on toxicity and further entrench polarised views. Yet, these same tools are packaged to us as useful, helpful and liberatory, and in the process we have become dependent on what they bring to our lives, whilst failing to critique how they harm us and our society.

Throughout my life, digital technology has actively impacted my mental health and wellbeing, and I have long felt at my core that something is not right. I have been trolled by men online, I have been stalked and harassed online, I have battled with body dysmorphia and my self-esteem since my early teens as a result of images I've consumed online. These experiences undeniably impacted me and are inextricably linked to my identity as a young woman, and what that brings with it. They have made me feel unsafe, and at times even more unsafe than I did in the offline world. For years, I assumed these were things I would get over with time and growth, and while frustrating and painful, it was my responsibility to choose how to react and to not let them define me.

Technology, as both a science and an industry, is often imbued with an authority and regarded as synonymous objectivity. It is seen as an unquestionable entity that stretches across our world, intangible and impartial. This idea that technology is fundamentally objective is also known as the view from nowhere. This view argues that technology is not influenced by anyone's view, but just exists as fact. I too viewed technology as neutral until 2022, when my life was changed forever. My life shifted the day I truly awoke to how harmful the digital world could be. My eyes were opened to the ways that our digital and material lives are now forever intertwined, and my perspective on our technology changed forever. In 2022, when I found out my sister Aimee had died, my world was suspended into stillness. No one should have to find out about the loss of a loved one from a total stranger knocking on your door. Nothing could ever prepare you for the pain that comes with losing a loved one suddenly. In the police investigation that followed, we discovered that Aimee had been on a toxic online forum that encourages to the point of pressuring people to take their own lives, and with a substance easily available through the click of a button, she was able to take her life. Aimee had become one of a countless number of often invisible victims of online harms, and this loss allowed me to see how dangerous the digital world we now take as a given can be.

My sister's story is not isolated nor is it rare; it is simply one of the more severe and shocking examples of digital technology failing us. Digital technology can impact all of our lives differently, and often it can be positive. Some people have made fortunes through their online lives; they may have found educational content that has changed their views entirely or become part of communities they would have never met offline. Growing up as a Gen Z, I can't count how many online friends I've made over the years, and how so many of these people are now some of the most important people in my life. However, there is light and dark in everything, and there is a side of tech that is insidious and can shake us at any stage of our life either directly or indirectly. My experience of having a loved one who has become a victim of online harms and others like it are happening regularly, and each day I have been working on this book I have learned of new real-life horror stories.

You may have heard of the devastating murder of teenager Brianna Ghey, a far-reaching story that left the nation horrified. In 2023, sixteen-year-old Brianna was brutally stabbed to death by two teenagers from her school who used the dark web to fantasise over torture and death, and communicated with each other online to plan their attack on Brianna.[2] The brutal murder of Brianna demonstrated the atrocious consequences of an unregulated digital world and the impact it can have on young people's safety and their mental health. Brianna's family and mine are united in a way we could never have envisaged – we are both bereaved families who've lost a loved one as a result of online harms. Following both of our losses, Esther Ghey and I have been part of Bereaved Families for Online Safety, a campaign group dedicated to fighting for a digital world so that it can become safer and highlighting the vital need for tech companies and governments to prevent further harm to people across the globe.

As it stands, these companies are cashing in on a crisis of our humanity, with young and vulnerable people being most at risk. But the problem isn't exclusively social media or smartphones themselves; one of the key problems is that platforms have been designed to keep us scrolling whatever the cost. If social media was designed to keep users safe, harmful content – be it self-harm or suicide content, racist and transphobic content, or content that promotes disordered eating – would not be accessible. Aimee and Brianna could still be here today, growing into courageous, resilient and happy young women. Rightly so, many parents are recognising the vital need for an intervention and are seeing the damage that can happen when we sleepwalk into a complacency around the tech we are now so used to. Just like me as I was growing up, they know something is not right. But parents shouldn't be alone in the fight for a better digital world; it's a battle we all have stakes in.

Now, I want to analyse where we have landed today with digital technology and social media. Our online world has opened unparalleled connections, innovations and opportunities to us. There is no doubt that there is positivity to be found in the developments in technology for many people throughout the globe. In the past thirty years, digital technology has transformed our lives and made them unrecognisable to our ancestors. We are able to do things that we never thought would be possible only a few decades ago. Assessing the digital world and its dominance today, I want to ask a crucial question: at what cost has all of this come? I want to bring human stories back to the heart of technology; to reawaken us in the real world to realise we have more power than we may have thought to decide on what the next chapter of the story of digital technology will be.

So far, no one has asked us, the users, whether we're happy with the invisible contract we've been unknowingly signed up to – the invisible contract that means we have no one to turn to but a chatbot or an online form when we experience online harm. The invisible contract that means tech CEOs make billions whilst our lives become simply data to endlessly extract from the process. I want us to become aware of the dangers that are already here and help to build empathy, agency and humanity in our online spaces because any one of us could fall victim to its darker side. Our rapidly changing digital world is putting more people at risk of harm each day. Whether it is being fired by an algorithm and losing your income overnight, losing a loved one after they consumed content that encourages self-harm, becoming obsessed with eating disorder content that further entrenches your own illness, or being digitally excluded when essential services become digital by default – online harms are not black and white. They are the daily realities, the frequent inconveniences, the growing burdens of a digital society that, until now, we have had little say in shaping. You've probably experienced online harms without even realising. Online harms are the risks, dangers and toxicities we experience online – what's vital to know is that they're preventable. The same way we create safeguards offline, be it seat-belt requirements or laws against hate crime, we have to have the same measures in place for our digital world.

In recent years, you might have noticed that tech leaders have joined the growing advocates who claim to want to uphold 'free speech'. On the surface, this can seem like a righteous aim, but beneath the veneer of libertarian attitudes is an insidious justification. Free speech is not a moral interest for Big Tech companies and their CEOs, it's a business interest, since extreme content gets more engagement, and more engagement means more profit. If tech leaders were to regulate so-called 'free speech', the foundations of their business model would be put at risk. Not only this but in today's digital dictatorship where tech companies are the stewards of whose voice is amplified and whose is silent, free speech becomes a fallacy in itself. Recognising this enables us to see more clearly that online safety is not a moral dilemma for tech leaders, but an economic one. It's a dilemma that pressures them to fundamentally challenge the business model that has earned them their billions. But instead of letting us get complacent, this should motivate us further to propel them into action. We have to ask ourselves, are these the people we want to become the unelected leaders of our modern world? People who – like Mark Zuckerberg who stood before bereaved families at the US senate in 2024 – can be faced with the devastation and pain of dozens of grieving families who have lost their children to the dangers on social media and *still* fail to act to prevent them?

This book is not going to be me telling you to stop using technology altogether, nor is it an academic or inaccessible investigation of Big Tech. In this book, I want to dig into the heart-rending and compelling human stories of those who are being impacted by the unwieldy world of digital tech. In writing this book, I interviewed voices like my own, who have felt entirely powerless to the unrelenting force of the companies that are not protecting us from online danger. I have attempted to include people from all walks of life, from a variety of backgrounds and demographics – from workers to women to teenagers and people of colour – to illustrate that despite our differences, we all have our own personal grievances with the digital world today. We all have stakes in this, and reclaiming our digital world is a collective fight. Throughout this book, I have included various lived experiences that might shock, upset or trigger you. This is not for shock factor, but is necessary in order for us to be able to understand how high the stakes are. Reclaiming the digital world doesn't just mean reclaiming our attention from the social media giants that steal it, an experience I'm sure you're familiar with. Reclaiming the digital world means ending the harms that are already happening and preventing future ones. The experiences in this book show just how urgent this is, and reveal the lived realities of our now digital lives.

Through these human experiences I will give my perspective on how we might be able to make a change, and where the responsibility for that change sits. Individuals are not data points or faceless entities to monetise no matter the cost. As my mum said in the days following my sister's death, 'If you bought a toaster and used it, but got electrocuted and died, that company would go under. Why are social media platforms any different?' Tech platforms have the duty of product safety, and it is something they are failing miserably at. Regulation is not a far-fetched ask nor is consumer safety a new concept, yet for Big Tech platforms, it remains something they've largely managed to avoid and outsource to users. This hypocrisy is not dissimilar from BP coming up with the carbon footprint, which has become a profitable cop-out, a tokenistic slogan they have created to shift the responsibility away from corporations and on to us. What is really required to turn the dial on climate change is action from those very fossil fuel giants that are cashing in on the climate crisis. It doesn't matter if we all cycle to work, if companies keep mining more oil we will continue on the path to destruction. Regulation has happened in the tobacco industry, the pharmaceutical industry, the gambling industry and the gaming industry – so why hasn't it reached the tech industry?

Every time I met someone to talk about my book during the research and writing process, I would tell them that learning how tech was evolving and the harms it was causing is how I imagined climate scientists felt in the 1970s when climate denial was common, a distant reality that wouldn't touch our lifetimes. For some reason, we seem to only realise problems exist once they impact us directly. Countries in the Global South have been feeling the impacts of climate change for years, while the Global North continues to extract oil, agree to new oil and gas licensing and live lifestyles which emit reckless levels of carbon emissions. It seems that only when there is a flood in your back garden that you may acknowledge the harms are not only real, but they are also already happening.

My concern is the collective cognitive dissonance that exists in modern culture. Perhaps closing off to these realities of our existence is a coping mechanism, but just like climate change, digital dangers aren't going anywhere, and they will only worsen with inaction. I don't want us to look back on this moment in time and ask ourselves why we didn't do anything. I don't want this era of immense technological innovation alongside devastating social harm to become a stain on human history, but unless we act to fix this, it will be exactly that. We can no longer sleepwalk into a future where the digital world becomes an unstoppable force, where its harms are accepted as normal, where its leaders are untouchable rulers, and where our lives are simply resources to be extracted, manipulated and profited from.

Technology is developing at a pace that the vast majority of us, and our lawmakers, cannot keep up with. Currently, it is activists and lived experience campaigners who are relentlessly firefighting against the sheer scale of online harms, while Big Tech companies add more fuel to the flames, sit back and line their pockets in the process. Governments speak of the appealing economic benefits of new technologies, while seeming to forget the human costs and emotional tolls. This book aims to bridge this gap in understanding, to be an antidote to the selective amnesia we see today, and document the stories of the people who are not being heard. As it stands, most of us have imposter syndrome when it comes to digital technology and before I wrote this book I did too. We feel that we can't speak on it as we aren't experts.

I've never considered myself a fan of technology. In school, ICT lessons were the thing I dreaded the most every week, and I have to get my younger cousin Erin to help me whenever I have tech issues. Like many of us, the unpredictability of tech often overwhelms me with panic, even after writing an entire book on this very topic. But as the users, the very people whose lives are shaped by our digital world, it's vital that we learn about *all* the ways that digital technology is shaping our lives, not just the stories of success. It's no use knowing ChatGPT is a tool without understanding how it might impact the future job security of creative professionals. It's all well and good knowing companies are becoming more efficient because of digital technologies, but not without knowing this is because algorithms are being used to fire workers if they aren't reaching unrealistically high targets and unreasonable deadlines. It's okay to scroll endlessly for hours if that's how you want to spend your time, but we should also understand the impact this is having on our mental wellbeing, attention spans and our relationships.

Techno-solutionism is the popular idea that technology can fix our problems, and it's the ideology responsible for much of the cultish hype we see around emerging technologies today, be it artificial intelligence or virtual reality. But what about when technology is fuelling or even creating the very problems preventing societal progress? In our increasingly digital world, we have developed a reluctance to accept that this is a possibility, let alone a reality. Looking at the world through this lens clouds our judgement and prevents us from progressing towards a better future for all. This is why the tech industry has for too long been treated as exceptional from the legislation that can keep us safe, because to regulate the digital world is falsely misunderstood as being anti-progress or anti-innovation.

Since losing my sister in 2022, I have invested countless hours in learning about the harms that the online world is fuelling. I have attended meetings with grieving families and tireless campaigners; I have heard from exhausted workers and burnt-out activists. In the meantime, tech CEOs have embarked on a new space race for dominance in what they see as the next best thing – artificial intelligence – whilst safeguards lag far behind. We are stuck in a cycle of repeating historical mistakes, of not taking the time to pause and ask ourselves whether these technologies are empowering or harmful, and if so, for whom? This book will shine a light on the ways that our current digital world fails, divides and harms us, and what the practical solutions are to reclaiming the digital world for the better.

If social media and digital technology is understood as an entire sphere in which we can not only participate in our world, but is becoming as important as the physical world, then why have we had such little say in creating it? The same way that our institutions are our people, so is tech – it is not some abstract force of nature but something we co-create. I hope that *Logging Off* will help you see that technology can never be neutral and so we can't be either. I want this book to compel you to act for the future and safety of those you love the most, to arm you with the knowledge to consider how you want to use digital tech moving forward and provide you with a new lens to see our world differently. We all deserve to lead happy, healthy and safe digital lives. We deserve our rights – be it our right to life, our right to decent working conditions, our right to thrive, our right to switch off, our right to live free from hatred and violence – to be upheld and respected. But as it stands, social media platforms and their addictive algorithms are preventing that from happening.

Logging Off is not just about spending more time offline or pouring ourselves into our lives beyond our online bubbles. It's also a rejection of the idea that we have to just accept things as they are. That online harms are just the other side of innovation and technological change. That they're inevitable consequences of a digital world that is still finding its footing. That's a myth that's been created by those who want to keep business running as usual, who are profiting from the crisis we're currently facing. With *Logging Off*, I hope to sound an alarm on why we urgently need a switch, why each of us has a vital role in remaking the digital world for our collective benefit and why Big Tech companies' power can no longer go unquestioned.

We all have stakes in reclaiming the digital world from Big Tech, because no matter who you are, the dominance of the digital world by corporations that only care about profit causes us all to lose out in our own lives, whether we lose out to our free time because we're being conditioned to be addicted to scrolling, or we lose agency over our work lives because our employer decides to replace our human bosses with algorithms. Or we lose the option to chat with a human about our health or banking, because public services have become digitised. Or like me, because we lose a loved one who has fallen down a rabbit hole of harm because the unregulated digital world has exposed them to new dangers and outdated legislation has failed to keep them safe. Humanity's capacity to destroy itself through our own innovations is nothing new, so how could we be bold enough to assume digital technology is any different? Our digital world needs reinventing. It wasn't done soon enough for Aimee and many others like her, but it could be reinvented for me, for you, and for anyone else who is logged on.

A note on language
In this book I will refrain from using the phrases 'the real world' in opposition to 'the digital world' as this implies that what happens in the digital sphere is separate from what happens in our physical lives, when in fact the online world is constantly changing and altering our realities beyond the screens. The online and offline world are now two sides of the same coin, and I will discuss them in tandem throughout this book, to reveal just how inseparable our lives now are from the digital sphere.

CHAPTER I

The Double Life of a Digital Native

'Fifteen years ago, the internet was an escape from the real world. Now, the real world is an escape from the internet.'
@noahpinion on Twitter, 2017[1]

I was born the year after Google was invented. I was nine when my sister and I first started playing The Sims. I was ten when my dad made my first Facebook account. I was eleven when I made my first YouTube video. I was twelve when I started photographing my clothes, posting them on Facebook and selling them in school before lessons began. I was thirteen when I first reblogged a photo of anorexic bodies on Tumblr because I thought that's what my body should look like. I was fourteen when I got my first iPhone. I was sixteen when I was photographed non-consensually by a man with his smartphone on a bus. I was eighteen when I got my first role as social media manager at a charity. I was nineteen when I was trolled on Twitter, which left me struggling with anxiety for years. I was twenty-two when I met my partner on Hinge. I was twenty-three when I lost my sister to online harms and my life changed forever.

As a Gen Z – part of the generation born between 1997 and 2012 – I grew up alongside the rise of the internet and the birth of social media. Some of my fondest memories as a child involve playing with my sister Aimee on our digital devices. Aimee was less than two years younger than me, and we were an inseparable pair. My mum dressed us in matching outfits and we didn't protest, despite how different we were. A running theme throughout our childhood was how much time we spent playing together. Not with Barbies, or toys, or out on the street like our parents, but online. We grew up playing Chadwick and the Sneaky Egg Thief, a pixelated colouring story game on the family Windows PC in the mornings, where Aimee would hide under the covers when the eerie start-up sound played. After school for years on end, we'd rush home for Aimee to load up Sims 1 and 2, where we'd be totally invested in the storylines of the Goth family and Aimee would design elaborate mansions and use the Motherlode hack for limitless cash to create the house of dreams. For her thirteenth birthday, Mum and Dad got Aimee an Xbox 360, and we'd play Assassin's Creed Revelations, boasting to our friends with pride about it being set in Istanbul. In the summer holidays in our mum's home town in Turkey, we would go to our friend Selin's house to use her computer to play Club Penguin and Stardoll since our grandparents have still today never installed Wi-Fi, and I'd mostly sit behind Aimee's shoulder and watch her immerse herself in this world I found both fascinating and intimidating. Mine and Aimee's childhood was framed by the golden age of the internet, when things felt full of possibility and it seemed that the advancement of the online world could only ever be a good thing.

Like most 21-year-olds today, my sister Aimee grew up spending a huge part of her life online. Her love for the music of Pharrell Williams and her vast collection of rare merch meant she delved into a part of the internet reserved for superfans like her. My mum and I would watch her get lost in her phone, scrolling for hours whilst we watched *Love Island*. Whilst she half paid attention to the heated drama on the TV, on her phone she was bidding for rare Billionaire Boys Club shoes and T-shirts on eBay with a fierce competitiveness, something that brought her incomparable satisfaction. With all of her purchases, she built an impressive archive that resembles a museum exhibit, and would self-shoot photo shoots in her room and around our house to post on Instagram and share with her wider fan community. Most people had never heard of Pharrell Williams until his *Despicable Me* hit 'Happy' graced our screens, but Aimee was not many people. As a teen, Aimee spent countless hours on Grindin', the unofficial forum for everything related to The Neptunes and N.E.R.D., bands Pharrell was a part of before he became a solo star. These digital spaces were a sanctuary where she could truly be herself and connect with fellow fans across the world who shared her passion, which was immensely important for her happiness at a time when school wasn't somewhere she could be herself. The online world opened Aimee up to an international community where she could express her passion without shame or judgement, and I will always be so grateful for each person she connected with for sharing that with her.

But in the same way that she found and became part of a community of Pharrell superfans online, she was able to discover other digital communities with different motivations too. If you've ever used social media, you will know that online, emotions are felt in their extremes. We are lonely and connected, we feel loved and hated, we feel optimistic and despairing, we feel informed and confused. This is the paradox that makes the digital world such a double-edged sword; it can be life-changing or life-threatening. When we are struggling with our mental wellbeing, we are more vulnerable to slipping down the rabbit hole. In a world where the technologies we use daily offer us a false illusion of connection, it is even easier to isolate ourselves from those we love. When Aimee was struggling with her mental health, we saw her spend more time in her room, away from her family and loved ones, locked into her digital devices. After we lost Aimee, I was shocked to discover that the risk of suicide-related outcomes among teen girls who spend more than five hours a day (vs one hour a day) on social media is increased by 66 per cent.[2]

During the Covid pandemic, Aimee struggled with the isolation and the mundane new normal that constant lockdowns had created. Like many of us, she wasn't able to do the things that brought her joy, like trying new restaurants with her boyfriend or travelling up to London to visit new exhibitions and her favourite art galleries. As a musician and devoted concertgoer, who had got herself on stage with Pharrell an impressive five times, the inability to experience music in its full form took a lot out of Aimee. These factors, combined with the addictive design of social media, made it easy for Aimee to isolate herself further. You've likely experienced this yourself at a point in your life; instead of putting down our devices and talking to someone for support, we stay logged on in a toxic cycle of comparison, depletion and hopelessness. Our offline lives become an overwhelming force we cannot bear to return to. This was what happened to Aimee. When she was at her lowest and most vulnerable, she got swept into a different path and fell down a rabbit hole online, which exposed her to harmful content and left her at the whim of dangerous and ill-intentioned strangers. She was vulnerable, and they knew that. More insidiously, she was given information and the encouragement to send her down a path she would never return from.

There are over 40,000 members and 2 million posts on the suicide forum that my sister Aimee found herself on. An investigation by the *New York Times* found that the site gains an average of 6 million page views a month – heartbreakingly, this is quadruple that of the National Suicide Prevention Lifeline.[3] Far from being a place reclined to the darkest corners of the internet, something you imagine would require insider knowledge and multiple hurdles to get to, it is as easily accessible as Facebook or eBay. The website founders claim that the site does not promote, encourage or aid suicide, yet they host a space where elaborate tutorials and methods are shared and promoted, where people plan and coordinate, whilst its creators evade any responsibility of the lives lost as a result. One in fifteen of us will at some point attempt suicide, and this is why having open conversations about the realities of suicidal ideation, depression and mental health is so important.

But this website isn't a safe space – it's a toxic breeding ground, where users are told to end their lives and instructed on how to do so by others. It is a space where despair is fuelled, and suicide is ridiculed, and spoken about as casually as a decision to buy a new jacket or book a holiday. Its users are told by strangers that their loved ones don't care about them, isolating them further and fuelling their loneliness. As Dr Matthew Nock, psychology professor and suicide researcher at Harvard University explains succinctly, being in this space when you're at your lowest is a recipe for disaster: 'It's like when someone's having road rage, handing them a gun.'[4] From just a few minutes of reading the posts, I feel physically depleted and anxious, and I can see just how easy it was for Aimee to get drawn into a space that she felt there was no return from.

In 2022, Aimee was found in a hotel room in a city sixty-three miles from her home town, with a stranger whom she had met on this suicide forum. The man who was with her had flown across the world to be there when she ended her life and he was with her in that same room for the eleven days before she did so. He was arrested on suspicion of assisting suicide but was later released on bail, after giving a no comment interview and having legal support throughout the process. I have spent hours trying to silence the painful thoughts of why he was there with her and how he could be the last person to speak to her. His presence made our pain tenfold. How could a total stranger be the last person to see her, speak to her, touch her? Would we ever know what exchanges they had on this forum, or how he influenced her when she was struggling most? Why did he not reach out to support services or her family once in those ten days, who might have been able to help her? The stranger who saw my sister at her most vulnerable has since returned to his normal life in America, without anything to answer for, whilst as a family we search for answers to the endless questions around the circumstances of the day that broke us. In the days after we lost Aimee, we were assured by police not to worry – 'he isn't some lowlife, he has a career,' as if that would ease our pain, or make his involvement any more innocent. Meanwhile, we had lost Aimee forever. This was all made possible by a toxic forum that capitalises on the despair and hopelessness of those who are in need of urgent support and fuels the insidious fantasies of sick-minded individuals at the same time.

Social media has created new opportunities for bad actors to prey on vulnerable people, groom and radicalise them into taking catastrophic paths. In 2023, the FBI issued an unprecedented warning about organised groups using social media platforms and messaging sites to target eight- to seventeen-year-olds, encouraging them to take part in acts of self-harm and suicide.[5] As a teenager, I experienced the gradual process of desensitisation to harmful content that happens online to young people every day. When I was fourteen, I unwillingly became a consumer of pro-ana (pro-anorexia) content when a close friend who was struggling with an eating disorder started resharing this type of content on Tumblr. Until then, I had never experienced body image issues. But within just weeks of seeing this content daily, I started to cut out food groups and despise my healthy adolescent body.

I would wish to be someone else, and I would spend hours urging my body to do what it couldn't and obsessing over depriving myself of the fuel it needed. Desensitisation is known to play a significant role in the psychological process of radicalisation.[6] We all know that we learn by seeing, and online, the infinite availability of information and content on any subject means we can become totally immersed in new worldviews in a matter of days. On the suicide forum that my sister found herself on, the constant exposure to conversations that underplayed suicide through jokes and glorification is something that puts suicidal and vulnerable people at more risk; it leaves them no room to see a way out. When I read through posts from users on the forum, I got a sense of the deep need for connection and support, but

I also got an insidious feeling that many of its users are there solely to spur on those who are vulnerable, and encourage them into making an irreversible decision. Sadistically, some users praise and encourage those who follow through with ending their lives, calling them heroes and legends. Knowing this fact makes it even harder to believe that the man who was present when Aimee died had her safety or wellbeing in mind, given he failed to alert any support services, despite being with her in that room for almost two weeks when she was at her most unwell. The desperation of some of the forum users for a way out can be understood just from reading a heart-breaking note left by former army cadet Joe Nihill, who took his life at twenty-three after being on the forum. It read: 'Please do your best in closing down that website for anyone else, look after my mum and family!'[7] If the very people that the forum claims to be supporting are calling for it to be closed down in their final moments, it's only right that we listen.

Aimee's death was not only fuelled by the life-threatening content that she saw on this suicide forum and the apparent assistance of a stranger, but also the fact that the poison that killed her was freely advertised and promoted on the forum. When Aimee was at her most vulnerable she was able to buy a deadly chemical with the same ease you might buy a second-hand top online or a new book from a high-street retailer. You can imagine the devastation we experienced as a family, learning that if this substance was not so easy to buy (at the time of writing, it is still available to buy on the world's largest online retailer website), she might still be here today.

My sister is not alone; there is a concerning trend of this chemical being promoted on suicide forums and bought online, being supplied by twisted individuals looking to profit from despair. There are bereaved families across the world who share the pain of my own family. Trillion-dollar company Amazon is currently facing a lawsuit from parents of sixteen-year-old Kristine Jonsson and seventeen-year-old Ethan McCarthy, who both bought 'suicide kits' on the site and used them to take their lives.[8] Until recent years, it was a substance virtually unheard of, but its promotion on suicide forums has led to the increase of fatalities from the chemical, particularly since the pandemic when so many were struggling with the social isolation that lockdown measures brought. In America, during the first eight months of 2022, there were fifty-six cases of human exposure to the chemical reported to poison centres, with twenty-five of them intentional.[9] However, eBay and Etsy have taken preventative action by banning the sale of the substance, but Amazon has failed to put safety first and is capitalising on the mental health crisis facing young people. As an industrial substance with legitimate uses, the government could easily regulate the sale of this substance by requiring buyers to have a controlled drugs licence. What seems like a small change could prevent vulnerable people like my sister from acquiring it, and save precious lives from future harm.

This is just one example of the growing chasm between the safeguards and protections that we have offline and online. As a 25-year-old woman, I have to regularly show my ID to buy painkillers, alcohol or dangerous tools such as knives. On the internet, risks persist which would be eradicated in an instance in the offline world. Imagine walking past a shop on the high street advertising suicide kits, with staff available to explain and promote the use of a chemical to end your life. The shop would likely last less than a day because of the public outrage at the immorality of targeting vulnerable people and profiting from their despair. Undoubtedly it would be closed down and the owner would face criminal charges under The Suicide Act for encouraging and assisting suicide. Online, nothing happens. Why not? What makes the online world exempt from the same protections, safeguards and moral standards that we recognise as fundamental to healthy and thriving societies? Is this not an absurd double standard, given that the average person in the UK spends six hours per day online?[10]

The failure of the British government to act on warnings from coroners and multiple police investigations has meant that the toxic forum that played a part in my sister's death has taken at least seventy lives in the UK, and it remains available to access at the time of writing. Governments in Australia, Germany and Italy have attempted to take action by blocking the site from domestic users, but loopholes mean many users can still access the site. It's now known that Kenneth Law, the man who was responsible for advertising and selling the substance via the forum my sister was on, is responsible for providing the chemical to at least ninety people who have died in the UK, including Aimee. Before his arrest by the Canadian authorities in 2023, he had sent over 1,200 packages of this poison across the world over a two-year period, preying on and profiting from people's vulnerabilities. Despite the nationwide calls to police from concerned families, Law's arrest only took place following the dedicated investigative work of *The Times'* social affairs editor James Beal, whose exposé led to Law's arrest and impending trial.

C.A. Goldberg is an American law firm representing sixty bereaved families that have been fighting to hold Big Tech companies to account for their role in deaths by this substance. One company they're fighting to sue for its complicity in the distribution and sale of this substance for use in suicide is Amazon. Amazon not only lists the substance, but actively promotes it to vulnerable users through its algorithm and recommendation features.[11] Carrie Goldberg, the founder of the law firm, tells me that despite her and bereaved loved ones writing to Amazon asking them to remove the deadly substance from its site, it remains the biggest seller of the substance. Instead of acting to protect people's lives, Amazon responded saying they had no legal reason to stop selling it, and even hired lawyers to defend their case, indicating their care for profit takes priority over people's lives.

Determined not to give in to the retail giant, C.A. Goldberg fought back, suing Amazon for its complicity in the sales of this toxic substance, and for the preventable deaths of far too many. After relentless lobbying to law-makers, C.A. Goldberg won legislative change that would prevent future deaths. California introduced Tyler's Law, named after seventeen-year-old victim Tyler Muhleman, which banned the sale of the substance for minors and would ban sales of a certain concentration to people over eighteen. The tireless work of C.A. Goldberg alongside the families who have lost loved ones proved that user safety is not difficult – it's just not a priority for these companies. This battle showed what is possible when there is the political will from those in power to keep us safe, and hold corporations to account for the harms that are fuelled by their platforms.

It would be foolish to talk about young people's mental wellbeing without acknowledging the impact of bullying. Smartphones and social media have made it even easier for children who bully to target people, ostracise them and harass them in new forms, often without a trace. From the rare instances of bullying I've experienced online, I can say that these experiences impact you so much more than people realise. The taunts stay with you, and the people's names remain ingrained in your mind for years on. Online bullying is downplayed and reduced to being content; it's just 'banter'. But cyberbullying has just as severe an impact as the bullying that happens in the corridors and the playground. The identities we develop as young people online are now parallel to our lived realities, and that is what makes online bullying so toxic.

As we will see in the following chapters, our online experiences drastically impact our mental wellbeing. For example, research has found that there is a link between being cyberbullied and visiting pro-suicide websites.[12] 'Be kind' can be seen as a tokenistic phrase, but it still holds weight because doing the opposite online can have severe consequences for young people and the trajectory of their lives. Given that suicide is the largest killer of under-thirties, and that experiencing bullying is closely associated with suicide,[13] tackling bullying behaviour is just as important as making the online world safe through laws and regulation. Ending bullying behaviour and tackling the complicity culture that we have around online harassment and bullying would help ensure that we prevent future loss of life and end the harms young people experience online.

When my sister passed, we were grieving a tragic and sudden loss. Separated across continents, with half of my family in Turkey, the grief felt interrupted and punctured by the constraints of time and space. Aimee was Muslim, and in Islam, you have daily prayers for seven days after a person's death, and we honoured this tradition. In the seven days after her death shook us all, women could be heard every evening for forty-five minutes reciting prayers in Arabic, the soft sobs from loved ones breaking up the hum of the soothing words. Seeing my grandma and the aunties who raised us sharing my pain, albeit through a screen, was a bittersweet relief that wouldn't have been possible without access to the internet and digital technology. Without digital technology, we would not have been able to grieve collectively as a family, transcending borders and crossing time zones to honour Aimee and her life. Digital technology isn't inherently bad, but in its current forms it is failing us.

Following what happened to Aimee, I became a part of a community that no one should ever have to join. Bereaved Families for Online Safety is a campaigning group of families who have all lost loved ones as a result of online harms. It is a grassroots group of parents and families who have come together and are united through their own losses in the fight for a better digital world. Until we lost Aimee, I had never heard of the group, nor had I heard of the legislation that they were fighting to secure, The Online Safety Act. The Online Safety Act 2023 is a new set of laws that aims to protect children and adults online, and it's been the focus of online safety campaigners in the UK in recent years. It puts a range of new duties on social media companies and search services, making them more responsible for their users' safety on their platforms.[14] Following Aimee's death, because of our personal experience of what catastrophic consequences can come as a result of a failure to regulate the online world in the same way we regulate the physical world, these laws became something I thought about daily.

On my twenty-fourth birthday in June 2023, I found myself in the House of Lords meeting the Bereaved Families for Online Safety group for the first time in person. Since I watched the Act being debated that day, sitting with the other bereaved families in the visitors' balcony, waiting with bated breath to hear from the decision-makers who would shape the future, The Online Safety Act has thankfully been passed into law as of August 2023. However, the work to bring its protections into effect will be lengthy and arduous, which is at odds with the rapid and ever-changing nature of the platforms it attempts to regulate. It's still unknown whether the forum that brought my sister into harm's way will be banned, or whether the founders will ever face consequences for the lives lost because of their toxic site. The criminal offences introduced by the Act include encouraging or assisting serious self-harm, cyberflashing, sending false information to cause non-trivial harm, threatening communications and intimate image abuse. While these are important developments, law-making is a slow and arduous process, whilst digital developments are the opposite. Legislation is failing to keep up. So how do we resolve this? We have to look at where the power lies to change things at the root cause, and that is with Big Tech companies. Their involvement, or lack of it, in safeguarding digital spaces is a key part of what I will cover in this book and has been a huge realisation for me since the loss of my sister.

It's not only the lack of safeguarding by tech companies fuelling the harms that so many are experiencing today. It's that social media platforms are designed to keep us logged on no matter the cost. Addictive algorithms do not direct vulnerable people away from harmful content, they keep pushing it our way, and this is the case for countless lives that have been lost to the dark side of the digital world. Addictive algorithms do not prioritise safety, they prioritise engagement. If our digital world was reinvented at the core, to prioritise user wellbeing and safety by design, the internet could easily be a place where people who are struggling with their mental health could feel uplifted, encouraged, hopeful about the future. It could exist as a space where they could be signposted to vital support, without judgement or shame, rather than a place that fuels their despair. With every premature death, there is a fight for justice to be had. My sister Aimee was curious, inquisitive and independent. But insidious actors – from the founders of the forum, to Kenneth Law, and the stranger who was present when she died – capitalised on this, and led her down rabbit holes that put her at risk of harm. The digital world isn't a matter of wrong place or wrong time – it is a system built with vast intent and purpose, designed to keep us glued to screens and engaged in whatever the algorithm sends our way. This is what led to us losing Aimee in dire circumstances that were not only beyond our control, but far beyond hers.

The emphasis I want to make is that my sister could have been anybody. She could have easily been you or one of your loved ones. She was a creative, unapologetic and stylish girl who loved Pharrell, Japanese culture and getting dressed up for meals out with her boyfriend. She was a keen traveller who could plan the most intricate itineraries for a city she had never stepped foot in from her diligent research. She was a humble artist who was talented beyond her years, inspired by the likes of Erykah Badu, Tyler the Creator, Basquiat, Kaytranada, Stevie Wonder and Sade. She was a sensitive and kind human being who had family and friends who deeply loved her. In her loneliest moments as a teenager, the online world was her saviour. In her loneliest moments, when she was mentally unwell, the online world led her to her death. My sister's story shows just how much the online world is a double-edged sword.

As it stands, we have no one to go to when tech harms us. Social media platforms are like black holes – they suck us in and swallow us whole, they work in mysterious ways, they intimidate us with their complexity. When their platforms do us more harm than good, they are simply untouchable, faceless apps that avoid any means of accountability. There is no recourse to justice beyond online forms that often go unread. Grieving families like mine are having to do their own investigations just to get answers about the circumstances of their loved ones' deaths.

Imagine trying to organise a funeral for your child whilst not knowing why they died. Imagine trying to grieve and having to fight to convince police to give you the information that might help you answer those questions. Imagine having to spend your grief fighting to make politicians pay attention. The traumatic experience of having to seek justice, jump through legal hoops and administrative hurdles, whilst you're still healing from a loss that you'll never fully recover from, a loss that could have been avoided, is incomparable. These are the real experiences of not just my family, but the families I'm now connected with, and many more whom I have not met but whose stories I have heard across the world. Meanwhile, tech companies move on unfazed, their profits untouched and reputations unscathed. At the time of writing this book, my family still do not know the conclusion of the criminal investigations into the circumstances of Aimee's death; we have still not yet had an inquest to get our answers, and it has been over two years.

About a year after my sister's passing, my mum came to me and told me that if she could say one thing to the man who was in the room when my sister died, it would be 'I accuse you of doing nothing.' We cannot do nothing. We can no longer delay collective action. We can no longer stand by and let the harms of the internet spill out and cost people their lives, and convince ourselves that these are rare incidents, freak accidents or 'one-offs'. We can no longer allow tech companies to treat people's lives and safety as collateral damage, or economic trade-offs. We can no longer keep viewing online safety as an individual choice, and instead as a fundamental right that tech companies must uphold.

I don't want anyone else to have to lose a loved one before they open their eyes to what is happening all around us. When you lose someone suddenly, you become very aware of your mortality and, as a result, much more conscious of how you want to spend your life and the kind of world you want to spend it in. Losing Aimee wasn't just a loss, it was a catalyst. It charged me into digging deep into the pain that we had gone through, and asking why and how this was able to happen. In a digital world that ought to connect and empower us, we hear now, at a worrying frequency, of families who are going through the torment of having lost a child who has fallen victim to the digital world's lack of protections and its relentless predatory forces. Since joining Bereaved Families for Online Safety, I've had the sad sense of being connected through a trauma that is going largely ignored each time a new family joins the group. And while death is the worst type of online harm you can experience, people are experiencing online harms every single day at a growing rate.

How is this allowed to happen? We must look to the companies who created this digital sphere to even begin to answer this question.

CHAPTER 2

Mining Your Business

'The data monarchs know more about me than my mother, my government or my doctor.'

will.i.am[1]

For us to understand how our digital world has come to be so dangerous, so toxic, so life-threatening, we have to first understand the business model that Big Tech companies operate under. I will use the phrase Big Tech as an umbrella term when discussing the tech companies that rule our modern world, including Meta (formerly Facebook and Instagram), X (formerly Twitter),* TikTok, Google, Amazon and Apple. While these are the companies I will be exploring in more depth throughout this book, it's not to say that other companies don't behave in this way too.

---

* The names Twitter and X are used interchangeably in this book. I use Twitter when writing about the site before its rebranding in July 2023, and X when writing about it since.

You likely already understand that under the global economic system of capitalism, resources become commodities to be monopolised, extracted and profited from, including our labour, land, housing and food. But the digital age has brought a new commodity into the mix: our data, our digital footprint and, ultimately, our intimate, emotional lives. Our emotional responses and day-to-day habits have become a resource that can be extracted, mined and profited from without our knowledge, and this is the raw material that has allowed the Big Tech empire to boom. Social media platforms would have you believe that they exist simply to connect us, that there are no strings attached. But the reality is something entirely different. Far from being free gifts, as users, we give just as much, in fact a lot more, to these social media platforms than they give us. We share, they take. Our attention is the natural resource that makes tech bros rich, not their tools or creations. So how did a handful of companies come to rule our modern lives by monetising our emotions and attention?

One cold winter evening in 2023, my friend Jo and I were driving home from a pickleball session she took me along to when she told me how she first got into it herself. 'I'd never even heard of pickleball before and then suddenly I started seeing clips of it on Instagram all the time.' She wasn't complaining; she simply found it baffling that her feed had suddenly started showing her this new sports craze, when Jo isn't a sports nerd. This is a phenomenon many of us social media users will have experienced. Almost overnight, our feeds will start to bombard us with a new stream of content. Often, it will feel eerily related to something you have said to someone as a passing mention, as if the technology around you had been listening.

Your devices are doing so much more than just listening. They are collecting vast amounts of information and they know how old we are, our gender, our race, our home address, our place of work, what we wear, whom we speak to and what our hobbies are. They know what stage of life we are likely in, if marriage or children are on the horizon, if we're single or in a relationship, and beyond this they even monitor our eye movements to track what content catches our attention best. This is just some of the information that is constantly being hoarded. But why? To sell. Our most personal information is being extracted and sold to data brokers and advertisers so that they can capture attention. It's hard to grasp just how intrusive this mining is, but there are moments when the façade slips.

One time when I was house sitting in Nottingham, I got an ad for Who Gives a Crap toilet roll on my Instagram stories, something that had never come up on my feed before and a product I had never seen or purchased before. It wasn't long before I realised the house I was staying in had this exact toilet roll. What felt like a spooky mystery was easily explained. In the guide the homeowner had sent me on WhatsApp, she let me know where I could find extra 'Who Gives a Crap toilet roll' and this data had been shared between platforms making my adverts personalised – or intrusive, depending on how you look at it.

What makes social media so valuable to advertisers is the ability to target individuals who can be influenced easily as they already have an affinity with the brand, or a need to satisfy, and the ability to personalise for this individual too. Imagine if each time you went into your favourite clothes shop, the rails were tailored with clothes they know you'd been complimenting on your friends, browsing online or admiring on influencers you follow. Your shopping experience would be totally different, and you'd likely leave with a lot more stuff you didn't need. By collecting vast amounts of data about who we are, platforms are able to make digital profiles of you, which advertisers benefit from. Scarily, Global Action Plan found that 820 million digital profiles of UK children are auctioned each day in order to sell ads.[2]

Data is now often described as the new oil, and this comparison is worthwhile. In their book *Data Grab*, authors Ulises A. Mejias and Nick Couldry argue that Big Tech companies and the predatory exploitation, expropriation and capitalisation of our information is a mutation of colonialism, which they call data colonialism. 'This latest seizure entails not the grabbing of land, but the grabbing of data . . . There is hardly a territory or activity that is beyond this kind of colonisation, and there is hardly a corner of the world that remains untouched by its technologies and platforms.'[3] Even the male, pale and stale demographic that makes up the tech barons is reminiscent of the colonial elite, the unelected leaders of the world who heralded themselves as the inventors of modernity and progress.

The messages we are fed paint a very different picture. These companies say that having this data about us is all to serve us better and to improve our lives. It's to make it easier for us, to make things more convenient, accessible too. They will never be honest about what monitoring our interactions, reactions, scrolls, taps, swipes and posts is truly for. Just like the colonisers of land, digital colonisation is an endless opportunity to make money. Without us, these platforms would be totally worthless. Our data might be an abstract and innocuous entity in our minds, but to the tech monarchs, it is the hottest commodity they could ever have got their hands on. With this immense amount of data, companies find it easy to make predictions about our behaviour, and therefore easier to influence us to act. This business model is what Shoshana Zuboff coined 'surveillance capitalism', and it is one that is becoming more intrusive and predatory with each technological innovation. These machinations make these companies billions, and the same actions are causing irreparable harm, to my sister and many others.

What does this Big Brother-esque business model mean for our lives offline, at a societal level? In 2018, an investigation by journalist Carole Cadwalladr broke that had the power to transform our understanding of social media's relationship with our personal data forever. The Cambridge Analytica scandal is the most infamous case of widespread unethical data harvesting by a renowned social media company. After whistle-blower Christopher Wiley went public, it was revealed that 87 million Facebook users had their personal data collected without their consent. By getting thousands of Facebook users to take a personality survey, data analytics company Cambridge Analytica were able to gain 5,000 data points on every American voter and predict their behaviour. Political parties across the world then hired the company to help them target voters with personalised political advertising. What once was limited to a universal brochure from your local MP through your letter box that your entire community received was now uniquely tailored to what this data revealed about you, and what type of political advert you might want to see.

Many of the political ads were deceitful, hateful and false. They made claims that fuelled the scapegoating of immigrants and Islamophobia. They spread lies that swayed huge numbers of voters ahead of the EU referendum and the 2016 US election. These ads played on people's vulnerabilities and susceptibilities and influenced their votes in two of the most significant votes in modern politics. As Christopher Wiley, former Cambridge Analytica employee, says, 'It's incorrect to call Cambridge Analytica a purely sort of data science company or an algorithm company – it is a full-service propaganda machine.'[4] It is no coincidence that Cambridge Analytica, the data analytics forum owned by billionaire Robert Mercer, was at the time headed by Trump's key adviser Steve Bannon. The scandal led to

Facebook's share price plunging by more than $119 billion, the largest ever share price drop in a company's market value in a single day.[5] But sadly, what ought to have been a moment of reckoning for everyone about how our data is exploited passed by. The momentum dwindled, anger dissipated and Facebook's dominance in our digital ecosystem went largely unchallenged, continuing to divide communities and threaten democracy.

Cases like Cambridge Analytica teach us why it is essential for us to understand that companies like Google and Facebook aren't just neutral service providers, they are businesses that will do what is in their financial interests. Google is not a library – it is an advertising company. Facebook is not a town hall – it is an advertising company. Instagram is not a photo album – it is an advertising company. For all the wealth that they extract from our society in the form of our data, Big Tech invests very little back into the communities that make their business possible. In the UK, TaxWatch found that the British arms of seven major tech firms including Google, Amazon, Meta and Apple paid only £750 million tax out of the £2.8 billion that was due.[6] They extract what they can from our personal lives, our information and our attention and give next to nothing back, while failing to keep users safe and society free from harm.

Ultimately, the motivation for profit underlies every action these companies take, and is the context for how they function within our society and our lives. Figures like Mark Zuckerberg, Elon Musk and Sam Altman are now household names who are granted privilege and power to pursue their economic interests. The economic dominance that Silicon Valley has established over our modern world and how we interact with each other grants these companies and their CEOs immense political power. Journalist Kara Swisher, who has reported on the business of the internet since 1994, compares Big Tech companies to nation states due to the sheer scale, power and force they have. Apple, for example, has a stock market size of $3.08 trillion, valuing it larger than the GDPs of all except six countries.[7]

With GDP as large as most countries, it is hardly surprising that these businesses hold immense lobbying power. Lobbying is when individuals or a group try to persuade people in parliament to support particular policies or campaigns. For corporations, policies that benefit them include things like lower taxes, softer regulation or protecting industries through things like government subsidies. Lobbying goes on largely behind the scenes and most of us will never know about the private meetings, expensive lunches and political back-scratching that goes on behind closed doors. In fact, social media companies invest millions into such sly favours each year to keep those in power on their side. A 2025 report by Balanced Economy Project revealed that Google, Amazon, Meta, Microsoft and Apple (GAMMA) top the list of companies for lobby spending in Europe, with all of them spending more on lobbying than the top ten companies in the financial sector or the automotive industry.[8] What this means is that our governments get bought out by Big Tech and decision-makers are incentivised to put the interests of these businesses over people. The users are cut out of the conversation and our influence on decision-making is minimised. It's urgent that we counter this pressure by electing politicians who will represent our interests and rights in the digital sphere.

While their lobbying continues to tailor our laws and legislation towards Big Tech's interests, these companies are also being shielded from the regulation that could protect the individual and save lives. Regulation is an essential tool that is applied to other industries that have a harmful societal impact, such as the tobacco and fossil fuel industry. It prevents companies from doing whatever they wish in the name of profit. As I explored the world of regulation, I came across Alexandra Pardal, the co-executive director of Digital Action, who formerly worked in corporate accountability relating to the fossil fuel industry. She told me that the failures we're seeing from Big Tech is part of the same problem we saw from fossil fuel companies in the twentieth century. 'It's taken decades of work building frameworks to hold fossil fuel companies to account and we are at the foot of the mountain when it comes to developing these frameworks for Big Tech now.' Big Tech platforms operate in the shadows, and Alexandra described that they are opaque in the way their products and algorithms work and how the companies operate globally, with high lobbying spends and low accountability. There is so much we don't know about these businesses and just like we've seen with climate change, sometimes we are too late to undo the damage these companies cause.

As it stands, Big Tech has an ego problem, one characterised by impunity and greed. They remain unchecked and unfazed, and society's view of tech as an unquestionable and exceptional thing is protecting them. Technochauvinism, a term coined by data journalism professor Meredith Broussard, is the belief that technology holds the answers to all our problems. It is a superiority complex that has characterised so much of Silicon Valley's ventures, and it has its forebears. During colonialism, Eurocentric views of the land as a resource to be dominated and commodified led to the extraction of fossil fuels and the eradication of indigenous people. Native knowledge of local ecosystems was looked down upon and actively erased as colonisers forced locals to assimilate and accept their way of doing things. This type of ignorance and binary thinking has led to unfathomable harm on many millions of people across the globe, and it is the same thinking that dominates the tech world and allows them to act as they wish. Narratives of 'innovation' and 'progress' cloud our judgement and make it harder to address the harms they are actively profiting from. The ego with which they operate obfuscates the industry's duty of care to its users. There needs to be more nuance in this conversation because tech companies are not beyond reproach, and neither should they be.

But there are challenges we face, especially when we recognise the monopolies Big Tech has over our digital lives. Each morning, you'll pick up your smartphone and scroll through the same social media platforms that your friends start their day with. You'll log on for work or studies and send important emails from Outlook or Gmail. You'll likely search any question that comes to mind on Google, or even ask your Alexa or Siri. These companies have quickly become household names and their products are daily essentials we can't imagine life without, and society has forever shifted in their favour. But with each day the world becomes more online, these companies increasingly resist changes to the exploitative business model that has amassed them billions. For these companies and their CEOs, change isn't just uncomfortable and disruptive, it isn't profitable.

We have to understand the motivations of Big Tech companies before we can even begin to challenge them. Moving forward, we should approach them with suspicion and mistrust for these companies do not simply wish to usher society forward towards progress. In this book I will trace a line from them to many different people who have been harmed, people who went from using these platforms with ease to feeling the direct impact in the worst possible way. I do this not as a fear tactic but to awaken you just like I have been awakened to the nefarious reality of tech we use day in and day out. Because far from what they'd have us believe, tech elites are not acting out of the kindness of their hearts or their desire for boundless innovation, but in fact to keep making profit at whatever cost.

CHAPTER 3

The Algorithm in the Room

Luke: 'What's an algorithm?'
Pete: 'It decides, it knows what you're thinking.'
Luke: 'How does it do that?'
Pete: 'It's an algorithm . . . that's what the algorithm does.'
Luke and Pete Talking Sheet[1]

If you are my age or older, you'll remember the old internet. This was a time before algorithms, when the internet was something you could dip in and out of as you pleased. It was something you used intentionally, whether that be to explore a personal interest or seek out like-minded communities. Sure, we surfed the web, but it required a level of work that the passive scrolling we do today doesn't. When social media was first born, our feeds used to give us updates in real time from friends and family, before the death of chronological feeds. Then algorithms took over, and our feeds became more intricate, a sophisticated web of content shown based on what the app believes you will be interested in. These algorithms are designed to drip-feed us an endless stream of content to keep us engaged and scrolling and because of the curation, they have created online bubbles, or echo chambers, in which we each exist online. Algorithms today are the culture makers, norm providers, thought leaders of our modern world. They influence where we go on holiday, whom we date, what jobs we apply for, what hobbies we take up and what politicians we vote for. But at what cost? Is this increased convenience and personalisation just an erasure of autonomy?

Big Tech's financial motivations have led to developments like algorithms, without any consideration as to how they might negatively impact our society. As our feeds are personalised, we become more disconnected, divided into a groupthink environment and severed from unity, nuance and room for debate. But what is this 'algorithm' we continually hear about? What is this faceless construct? It is hard to understand and often we don't know how an algorithm has been designed, how it works or what data helped to build it. And yet, they decide all of the content we see and engage with. On paper, an algorithm is defined as a set of mathematical instructions or rules that, especially if given to a computer, will help to calculate an answer to a problem.[2] But in practice, the lived reality is something quite different.

To appreciate how algorithms work in our daily lives, I want you to try an experiment. With a loved one, be it your child, partner or parent, swap devices and spend ten minutes scrolling through their most-loved apps. Whether it's their Facebook feed or For You page on TikTok, you'll rapidly get a sense of what it means to dive into another person's digital landscape, and you will soon realise that we each exist in our own unique bubbles online. You'll likely see content you'd never see on your own feeds, even though you might like to. You might even see something that shocks or upsets you. This experiment should help you realise just how much social media algorithms are disconnecting us from each other, but more than this, algorithms are breeding divisions and fuelling polarisation. An example of this is that the impact of these algorithms is reported as one of the reasons that Gen Z men and women have more polarised beliefs on the impacts of feminism.[3] This is because of so-called recommender systems, a design feature adopted by social media that determines what users see, based on their interactions with the platform. So instead of bringing people together, by highlighting a diverse range of experiences and exposing us to different perspectives, we are being fed information that supports our current worldview, and being pushed further away from those who disagree.

General elections are the perfect example of how this plays out in the world. In 2019 we were on the precipice of change. Standing to be elected was the governing Conservative Party led by Boris Johnson and the Labour Party led by Jeremy Corbyn, a politician and activist who would certainly have shifted the priorities of government immensely if he were to have been elected. During the run-up to the election, I would spend at least an hour scrolling through videos on Twitter that revealed the shocking and cruel legacy of Tory austerity and read articles from dedicated journalists who were dissecting and lamenting Conservative leadership and Boris Johnson's political history. On my feed, a chorus of voices echoed my own views that another world was possible, and that our compassion and shared realities could triumph over hate and division. I felt hopeful for change, and I believed the tide could turn and we could see the Labour Party elected.

But my social media feeds were an echo chamber of mirrors that held up my own political beliefs and moral values to me and convinced me that the majority of people felt the same. Meanwhile, another story was playing out that I was hardly aware of, one that wanted Boris Johnson to come into power and withdraw the UK from the EU once and for all. When I woke up to a landslide Tory victory on that gloomy Thursday morning in December, it led me to question how I could have got it so wrong. 'The distortions we experience viewing the world through these platforms are ideal for fooling people into thinking there is more support for their positions and wishes than there might otherwise be,' as the cultural historian Siva Vaidhyanathan expertly puts it.[4] My newsfeeds weren't simply keeping me informed as many of us think they are, they were showing me what I wanted to see, asserting my own views back to me and keeping me blissfully ignorant and unprepared in the process. Even the innocuous phrase 'newsfeed' is a misrepresentation; 'Youfeed' would be much more accurate. I'm always taken aback when I mention recent news to my parents, usually a subject that has been taking up my entire X feed for the past week, whether it's the latest Westminster scandal or Just Stop Oil activist stunt, and they've not heard it mentioned once in the news. Social media is not merely a new form of information access, it's a tailored diet of content curated to hold our attention.

So we are being siphoned off and divided, influenced and guided by these powers of technology that most of us don't understand. The algorithms that do so are designed by humans of a particular demographic and world experience, and so inherently they are biased to a certain perspective. There is no doubt that we cannot fully trust what we see, but how does that cause harm in our physical lives? How does it lead us to danger or risks offline? The key detail is that these algorithms that rule our feeds today are not designed to distinguish between what is good or bad, harmful or helpful, true or false, legal or illegal. Instead, they're designed to keep our attention captive. As a result, we are exposed to what the algorithm thinks we might want to see or might spark our curiosity, no matter what that is. The fact that everyone's feed is totally different is what makes it so much harder to realise the scale of harmful content that is out there, but it is out there and being fed to those who are vulnerable.

The recommender systems that are used by social media giants today analyse our behaviours and lead us down rabbit holes of harm. They are not designed to have the discernment or empathy that humans have intrinsically, they are created to keep us locked in and online. The Center for Countering Digital Hate found that within 2.6 minutes, TikTok recommended suicide content to accounts registered as thirteen years old.[5] On top of this, researchers from Amnesty International found that with each hour spent on TikTok's 'For You' feed on dummy accounts created as teenage girls, more of the video clips 'recommended' to the teenage account show children and young people crying, or alone in the dark overlaid with text expressing depressive thoughts or faceless voices describing their suffering, self-harm and suicidal thoughts.[6] Such evidence is clear: people are being shown dangerous content, often at a time when what they need most is to be signposted towards support or shown things that might uplift them and offer hope.

Alice Hendy MBE has seen this play out in her own life. Tragically, she lost her brother Josh to suicide when he was just twenty-one and devastatingly, Alice learned that Josh had been consuming harmful online content before he died. Alice asked herself the same questions that I did after we lost Aimee: why didn't these social media platforms pick up on this and signpost Josh towards support? Alice was motivated to change this reality, and her experience led her to create R;pple, a secure and confidential interceptive tool designed to help individuals searching for harmful content online. The tool can be downloaded on to digital devices and it can recognise and signpost those in need to vital mental health support when they search for harmful content, diverting them away from content that puts them at risk of harm. Already, twenty-four individuals have come to Alice to say they're still here because of R;pple's intervention, revealing the transformative power of tech tools designed for social good and with our wellbeing in mind. In the algorithmic age, the phrase 'prevention over cure' has taken on a new meaning entirely, one that can have life-saving consequences.

This algorithmic dictatorship isn't the digital future that young people want; a 2024 survey of more than half a million eleven- to eighteen-year-olds in the UK found that mental health and wellbeing was their biggest concern.[7] In the US, school districts are filing lawsuits against social media giants for their addictive algorithms, design features that are fuelling the mental health crisis in young people.[8] Each day, it's becoming clearer that young people are in a battle against Big Tech's addictive design, and in many cases, logging off is becoming their only viable option.

Algorithms not only determine what we see, but what we don't see. The fact that social media platforms and their algorithms do not simply show us what we want to see, but actively reproduce gaps in our knowledge was made clear to me during the humanitarian crisis in Gaza, which escalated in October 2023. On 7 October 2023, more than 1,000 people were killed and over 200 taken hostage in Israel by Hamas, resulting in an assault on Gaza from the Israel Defense Forces, which has killed more than 40,000 people in Palestine in violence that has lasted over a year.[9] A 51-page report by Human Rights Watch found that Meta was systematically censoring voices of Palestinian solidarity, since hostilities between Israeli forces and Palestinian armed groups escalated on 7 October 2023.[10] If you had shared something about Palestine on social media and ever wondered why you hardly got any views, likes or shares, it's likely that this algorithmic censorship was the cause.

Between October and November 2023, Human Rights Watch found 1,050 cases of algorithmic censorship, whether suspending or banning accounts, removing content or restricting users' ability to interact with others' posts, and shadowbanning. This mirrors a historical pattern of ingrained bias in favour of Israeli political narratives at Meta, formerly Facebook. In 2017, a series of internal documents from the company were leaked, which revealed the ways that the company's content moderation is biased towards suppressing Palestinian voices. Meanwhile, under Facebook policy for its abuse standards, it was found that Zionists are listed alongside 'vulnerable' groups; 'homeless' people and 'foreigners' are also included within this classification. However, 'migrants' are only semi-protected, and 'Black children' are not protected at all.[11]

What this means is that embedded within Facebook policy is positive discrimination towards Zionist ideology, however, advocating for the right for Palestinians to live in peace and free from occupation could get your account censored. There were methods innovated to resist this censorship, such as slotting selfies between infographics, sharing screenshots of resources rather than direct reshares, or using symbols instead of letters (Fr33 P@l3stin3, for example). This language adaptation to circumvent algorithmic censorship is so essential it even has a name: algospeak. Social media platforms are not apolitical spaces designed for freedom of expression. They were not designed with civic participation in mind, and it's for this reason that they determine whose voice is amplified and who gets silenced.

At a time when so much of our civic participation is influenced by injustices we see online, as we saw during the rise of the Black Lives Matter movement in 2020, algorithmic censorship can stifle resistance and solidarity. But people continue to fight back in the digital age and make space for the issues they care about beyond what the algorithms show us. When Malaysian kids who were too young to attend offline protests organised a Palestinian solidarity protest on the multiplayer gaming platform Roblox with their avatars carrying Palestinian flags and signs that translated to 'Solidarity for you', it was a demonstration of how children carve out spaces for civic participation in their online communities.[12] Palestinians also took to Queering the Map, a digital map which allows

LGBTQ people to submit anonymous geotagged posts from places of memory, to share their memories of love, loss and heartbreak with the world. In solidarity, The Dyke Project hacked 100 adverts across Transport for London to share queer Palestinian voices and amplify their stories, at a time when they were being actively erased.[13] These are all examples of us collectively reclaiming digital technology for the collective, and demonstrate the radical potential of our imagination and creativity in the digital age.

Algorithms are impacting our society beyond the social media feed too. They're now used in almost every field, to make predictions, calculations and influence decisions in relation to our lives. That includes industries like policing, work, healthcare and education. Computer scientist Joy Buolamwini knows this all too well, but it took an experience that shook her to her core to learn just how intrusive these algorithms have become, and how far-reaching their impacts are. Joy was over the moon when she got accepted into her dream university, as a scholar at MIT Media Lab. Her fascination with computers and artificial intelligence stemmed from childhood; undeniably gifted, she taught herself XHTML, JavaScript and PHP at the humble age of nine years old. Joy's path could be considered the poster child for STEM success and now, joining a renowned institution pioneering technological innovation and forward thinking, she was embarking on a huge step in her career. But this achievement was not the life-defining moment that she had hoped for. What came next was a series of events that changed her outlook on technology and opened her eyes to the bias that is ingrained in its very foundations.

In her first year of the graduate course, her class was assigned a project to create a new technology inspired by science fiction and personal curiosity. Joy decided to invent the Aspire Mirror, which would use artificial intelligence to layer an aspirational figure's face over your own (her own being Serena Williams). Drawing from existing code to design facial recognition software for her own creation, she combined her personal vision and interests with existing resources to build a new technology. But when she attempted to use the prototype, she was confronted with a shocking revelation: the mirror didn't detect her face. Was it merely a glitch? A lag in the system? The classic prototype problem? These could have been the reasons, but when Joy decided to test a suspicion that was ruminating in the back of her mind, she was confronted by a sinister reality. When she held a white mask over her own face in the reflection, the Aspire Mirror finally lit up. Now, masked behind white plastic, it registered her existence. This ingrained bias in digital technologies is what Joy went on to call 'the coded gaze'. It led her to a pursuit of unravelling artificial intelligence and algorithmic bias, digging beyond the surface of neutrality and innovation that we assume as being unflinchingly accurate.

Joy went on to collaborate on pioneering research alongside fellow computer scientists Timnit Gebru and Deborah Raji. Their paper 'Gender Shades' was revolutionary, and led to a monumental shift of the dial in how the tech industry is understood, making its shortcomings known. The research found that leading tech companies' technologies routinely misgender women and dark-skinned people, and in some circumstances did not even detect dark-skinned faces at all. Astoundingly, the failure rate for dark-skinned women was over one in three, whilst pale male data (images of white men) were detected with no errors.[14] This was a glaring revelation of the racism that was wound into the fabric of the digital technologies that were supposedly going to innovate and change our world for the better.

You might conclude that these are simply teething problems, limited to new technologies that haven't yet found their feet. But in 2011, the personal experience of another Black woman in tech revealed that this bias is as mainstream as the internet itself. It was a week-end of parenting duties, and Safiya Noble was looking after her stepdaughter and her cousins. Reluctant to let them spend the day watching crap TV and mindlessly scrolling but needing inspiration, she decided to search for things that young Black girls growing up in Illinois might be interested in. On Google, she typed 'Black girls' and hit search, expecting to be met with suggestions of child-friendly activities or youth organisations nearby. But Safiya was horrified to see the engine had presented her with a deeply inappropriate and racist result. The hits were a barrage of porn websites. The world's biggest search engine had reduced Black girls and women to their bodies and sexuality within a second.

Her dedicated research into search engine algorithms since that day has revealed that search engines are not simply a digital version of the Yellow Pages we used to flick through to find anything and everything we needed. In reality, search engines and their mysterious algorithms reflect the biases of their creators, and the inequities of our systems are ingrained within them. Noble coined this the 'Algorithms of Oppression' and other examples of this at play included when Google Images tagged an African American couple as gorillas,[15] and a Google Maps search for the N-word directed users to the White House during the Obama presidency.[16]

These are not simply 'glitches' but fundamentally reveal how technologies – the very technologies that now define the bounds of innovation and societal progress – are never objective. Consider for a moment the fact that Siri, Alexa, Cortana and all other voice assistants have women's voices. Is it purely a coincidence that a product designed to represent unfettered subservience and around the clock assistance is modelled to have the name and voice of a woman, while the vast majority of tech companies are dominated by men? Even UNESCO has raised the alarm on this phenomenon; a report in 2019 found that voice assistants projected as young women reinforce harmful gender biases which reproduce gender inequality.[17] On our feeds, the age-old pattern of gender inequality repeats itself. The NPC trend, which saw women streaming on TikTok live, robotically acting out orders and gestures at any command like a GTA avatar, was just another manifestation of the bias at the core of our digital world. As content creator @masonelle on TikTok asks, 'To reduce woman to a machine. Is this not the technoindustrial fantasy?'

It goes further than this. As algorithms come to be used by police to identify suspects, doctors to identify tumours, governments to detect benefit fraud, their biases are profoundly impacting our material lives, whilst the use of these technologies over human decision-making goes largely unquestioned. The inequalities that persist in our material world become inscribed into the digital technologies we now use, reinforcing and amplifying them. In 2020, non-profit Foxglove exposed that the government's algorithm, which graded A levels during the pandemic, was marking down students from disadvantaged schools, revealing how historical human biases become institutionalised into these computer processes.[18] What could have ended up depriving children of the potential to pursue their dream careers and attend higher education was only prevented because of student grassroots action. After mass student protests the government ditched the flawed algorithm, and teachers' grades were used instead, but this could have easily limited an entire generation's future prospects, simply because of their class background.

Similarly, the use of algorithms and artificial intelligence in facial recognition technology are fuelling the racist profiling that activists and racialised communities have been fighting to end for decades. Research by Big Brother Watch found that six out of seven matches by the Metropolitan Police's live facial recognition technology have been false matches, and people of colour are at significantly higher risk.[19] In 2023, African American woman Porcha Woodruff was eight months pregnant when she was wrongly arrested by six police officers at her home address for robbery and carjacking after the use of AI facial recognition technology, which falsely identified her as a criminal.[20] The stress that this likely had on her, just a month away from giving birth, would have undoubtedly been immense, putting both her and her baby at risk of harm. These are the very inequalities that activists and campaigners offline have been fighting to end for years, and they are now being reversed by the use of algorithms and automated decision-making processes that are assumed to be superior to human knowledge.

The lack of accountability when algorithms are used to make decisions instead of people is a paradox that is only fuelling the problem. For the vast majority of us, this dilemma means we have no one to turn to for help when we've been a victim of algorithmic discrimination or bias, with those in power simply claiming these to be freak accidents or one-offs. But this is a problem at the core of the techno-solutionism that rules our world today.

'The public sector is really vulnerable to sales pitches from these tech companies who come in and say, "Look, you haven't got much money; we'll give you an algorithm and we can make all your problems go away." Facial recognition technology is comparatively cheaper than it is to invest in police officers who can actually respond to

crimes, investigate and make people feel safe,' says Made-
leine Stone, senior advocacy officer at Big Brother Watch.

For the companies selling this technology, it's a benefit
to be able to avert criticism and scrutiny for their failures.
As Sundar Pichai, CEO of Google and Alphabet, told one
interviewer, 'No one in the field has solved the hallucina-
tions yet.'[21] Meanwhile, local communities pay the price
of the introduction of these tools. Between 2016 and 2018,
eight trials by the Metropolitan Police resulted in a 96 per
cent rate of false positives, with a fourteen-year-old boy
among those wrongly identified and then fingerprinted
as a result.[22] Big Tech companies are very well aware of
the societal harms their products are creating, but are
reluctant to resolve them because to do so would be costly
and would dispel the myth that they have worked so hard
to create in popular imagination: that these companies
and their products are beyond scrutiny.

Algorithms calculate averages, predict outcomes and
can help make decisions more quickly, but human lives
don't work in averages; we are much more complicated
than that. Algorithmic bias combined with an unquestioned faith in technology over human judgement can
end up having the opposite effect of what services aimed
to keep people safe, educate and care for people are
designed for. Algorithms are not some ethereal cog in
the technological system; they are shaping our daily lives
and futures in ways beyond our control. After years of
austerity and cuts to public funding which have resulted
in a public sector that is in collapse, shiny new tools can

seem like a quick fix. Tech companies are happy to have us vest our hopes and money in their products, seeing them as a silver bullet to our societal problems.

Outsourcing complex decision-making to artificial intelligence and algorithms might mean we get decisions made faster, but when these decisions are the wrong ones, we need to ask ourselves what is more important. You only have to look at the experiences of sub-postmasters and their families during the Post Office scandal to understand that implementing technologies on a vast scale before we have done the due diligence to ensure they are effective and safe can ruin lives and scar communities beyond comprehension, and this is discussed in more detail in Chapter 9. Whilst algorithms and machines might be cheaper and faster at making decisions, they are not better equipped than human judgement and collaboration. Instead of making service provision digital, we ought to ask ourselves first if this is the future we want, or that tech companies want. Digital technologies should be used to enhance our capabilities, not hinder them.

Someone who is trying to address this at the root is Sneha Revanur. At the age of fifteen she founded Encode Justice, the world's first youth advocacy group specialising in artificial intelligence, in response to a policy in California that would replace the use of money bail with the use of an algorithm instead. Recognising the harm that this could pose to racialised communities, she launched a campaign to get the policy ditched, a campaign which led to a victory for the community. Today, Encode Justice is empowering young people across the globe to hold their representatives to account, and demand that algorithms and artificial intelligence be used and integrated with future generations in mind.

Algorithms profile us and squeeze us into neat stereotypical boxes, they steer us to things we don't want to see and obfuscate things we do want to see. They make decisions for us and feed us a diet of content that aligns with the predictions they've made about us, one that reduces our lives to data points. You don't realise what images teen girls are seeing unless you are one. You don't realise how widespread misogynistic views have become among young men and boys unless your algorithm has calculated that this content might be of interest to you. You forget that climate denial is a deeply entrenched conspiracy which has thousands of people in its grasp, until you lose a loved one down the rabbit hole. You're more likely to be shown content that encourages you to end your life if you're already vulnerable. As a result, we live in single issue bubbles online (to paraphrase Audre Lorde), blissfully unaware of each other's vulnerabilities until someone you know and love acts on them. This is the real-life consequence of addictive algorithms, and we all lose out. This invisible process grants social media companies immense power, power that enables them to determine our futures. Social media giants have become thought leaders, with their algorithms determining collective attitudes to issues such as feminism, migration, racism, climate change and public health.

But algorithms aren't some mystical force, they're highly sophisticated computational processes that work with numbers and data. They seem immaterial, beyond our reach, but in many ways they're one of the most powerful hidden forces shaping the trajectories of our modern lives and are being used to determine everything – from what we see on social media to whether we get fired or hired, to whom police decide to arrest, yet for most of us, our understanding of them remains limited. This is an understanding that multi-million-dollar tech companies would rather you didn't have. Knowledge is power, and in the digital age, the gatekeeping of knowledge by tech companies actively disempowers us from voicing our concerns and speaking up against the unfair use of digital technology. Understanding how algorithms are being used to make decisions all around us is the first step towards change. We have to question the power that tech companies have been granted. The alternative is to be blissfully ignorant to the harm that happens all around us, until that harm impacts you directly, something I wouldn't wish upon anyone.

CHAPTER 4

Social Media as the Slot Machine

'The short-term, dopamine-driven feedback loops that we have created are destroying how society works.'
Chamath Palihapitiya, former VP of user growth at
Facebook[1]

Social media has become an addiction many of us are contending with every day. As we've learned, algorithms capture our attention and lock us in. And since the rise of the smartphone, we now have access to the online world no matter where we go. We are trapped in a toxic cycle of consumption, validation and instant gratification, and our brains are lapping it up. But how bad is it? And what does this mean for our brains and wellbeing?

I once saw a viral TikTok video that sums up our relationship with social media today. The video showed a clip of a young woman prancing in a big garden surrounded by birdsong. She is smiling and spinning without a care in the world. She is completely and euphorically present.

But then I noticed the caption which read, 'me during the ten seconds of my phone restarting'. When I saw it I laughed out loud but deep down I felt disturbed that so many of us have this type of dependent relationship with our digital devices, so much so that our only break from them is when they run out of battery or when we sleep. Being present is now a rare feeling and one that I struggle to feel myself.

Boredom is not an emotion we regularly experience any more as there is always something on our phones to keep us occupied. I spend most of my time immersed in a screen or a book, or switching between the two. Most of us keep our phones next to us every second of the day: they sleep with us, eat with us, go to the loo with us. Any time you're on public transport during rush hour and look around you, you can see the trance-like state of almost every person locked into a screen. It feels like something out of *Black Mirror*. As much as many parents begrudge the 'antisocial' tendencies of Gen Z and younger generations, most of us didn't choose to be this way. None of us want to be addicted to our devices. We may give in to it, yes. But I think most people would say they want to experience things in real life, not through the rectangular screen in their hand. The truth is we have become the guinea pigs of the online world and the tech overlords who built it, and psychologically we are all suffering the consequences.

It is undeniable that the smartphone has made digital addiction more prevalent than other innovations, but how is it different from other devices? The potential for it to be used anywhere is seen as a gift, but it is this which makes the smartphone all-consuming. Desktop PCs or televisions don't travel in our pockets, detect and predict our behaviours and movements, or influence us to continue watching or flicking through channels. I have faint memories of when the internet was a space reserved to a corner of our house, a time before dinner, after school or work. Fundamentally, logging on was an intentional choice, something that we took part in during a certain time frame, but there were situational restrictions on usage. Smartphones on the other hand offer an endless stream of opportunities for distraction and as devices they have come to be inseparable from not only our bodies but our minds. Today, mindless scrolling has most of us in a chokehold. I understand implicitly that it's bad for me, but a quick scroll and scan of my emails and social media notifications is still the first thing I do when I wake up, no matter how hard I try to resist the urge. Logging off can feel impossible. But what makes our phones so irresistible? In order to understand why we just can't stop scrolling, we need to understand the design of our digital world and that requires an introduction to some basic psychology.

Intermittent variable reinforcement is the psychological model that slot machines are designed on, and this is the same model social media apps are designed on too.[2] This psychological process gives us rewards for our behaviour in unpredictable frequencies. In the 1950s, psychologist B. F. Skinner observed that lab mice responded most voraciously to random rewards, compared to lab mice that would receive the same reward every time they pressed a lever. The mice that received unpredictable rewards and sometimes none would press the lever more compulsively.[3] In the case of social media platforms, the rewards that keep us logged on and locked in are notifications and alerts. We are primed and conditioned by design to act out behaviours (scrolling, liking, commenting) in the hope of getting a reward that we don't know what it will be. The inconsistency is what keeps us coming back. TikTok has mastered the art of this. The vast majority of my For You page isn't of interest, but still, I'll keep scrolling in the hope of getting lucky. In the case that I do see a video that interests, inspires or excites me, I unconsciously get a hit, which incentivises me to keep scrolling for more. Social media promotes a culture of bingeing because its design features – such as infinite scroll and autoplay – are created with the very purpose of addicting us.

Content bingeing is something many of us experience. After a day offline, I will manically scroll through what I've missed, not fully appreciating what I'm looking at. Flying through posts and videos I am not critically engaging with, I am being passively entertained, and when I'm not, I swipe. When you don't give in to this bingeing, often you fear you could be missing out on something important, or as soon as you are a tiny bit bored, this content feels like it's the easiest solution. And while this scrolling can seem harmless, the reality is bleak. The same way that the only consequence of working more is more work, the only consequence of scrolling more is more scrolling, and more scrolling fatigue as a result.

The scientific research proves how harmful our addiction can be; MRI scans have shown that heavy users of Facebook develop poor attention, impulsivity and brain patterns that look like ADHD.[4] I've noticed as I've grown into my mid-twenties that it feels like I have next to no control over where my mind wanders. I feel constantly alert, unable to switch off and relax, worried that there's something I'm forgetting to do. I even sought an ADHD diagnosis, to no avail. Now I suspect that what I thought was ADHD is actually the long-term result of growing up accustomed to a bombardment of notifications that demand I pay immediate attention to, all of them pressing me to view them as equally urgent. A recent study of college students found that they can only now focus on any task for sixty-five seconds.[5] Younger people's brains are more vulnerable to the psychological effects of this type of information, since they are still developing, with Dr Porter stating that 'the current generation of young adults are treating their brains more like a search engine than a traditional fact retrieval system.'[6] The insidiously addictive nature of endless access to short-form content and its impacts on our attention span now even has a name – TikTok brain.

Social media is addictive by design, leading us to be hypersensitive to approval and validation. Beyond this, it impacts brain development in young people, gives us poorer cognitive performance and it can contribute to anxiety, depression and isolation. The mental health crisis is a huge part of the conversation around social media usage that continues to come up in public discourse. The continual comparison to lives online is prompting many to feel depressed about their lives and experiences, and consistent connection online is not the same as real-world human connection, and can make us feel lonely and dissatisfied. Research shows that limiting social media use to just thirty minutes each day can lead to significant reductions in symptoms of loneliness and depression.[7] Furthermore, 92 per cent of parents think social media/ the internet is having a negative impact on their children's mental health.[8] The research and evidence are clear on how bad these devices and the platforms they host can be for us, and yet we keep coming back for more.

Something I realised when I went on my first girls' trip to celebrate my twenty-fifth birthday was that every single one of us had tried to limit our social media use and content consumption. Each and every one of us was fed up with the mental exhaustion and overwhelm that had accompanied growing up online. We all had different tactics: India would go on long walks without her phone; Romalie was embarking on her first year off social media; I would use an app called Opal to block apps for certain periods of time each day; Makena would delete apps as and when she needed a break. Makena told me that same week that social media now feels like a job; the sense of pressure to be visible has become a constant in the back of her mind. This is a reality and dilemma so many of us are facing. Our digital double lives are becoming burdens on our mental wellbeing and a source of stress instead of something we can just pick up and put down at ease.

Instead of being something we actually want to do, we have all got invisible strings that keep drawing us back to these devices and the infinite amount of content they contain. We are not simply distracted because this would suggest that this is a minor inconvenience, a background feature of our lives. Author Maggie Jackson believes that social media platforms have established an institution-alised culture of interruption. The reality is that we are being dictated to and dominated by digital metrics. Noti-fications, daily streaks, sensational newsfeeds and alerts all hack our brains and compete for our dwindling capacity to pay attention. We spend boundless time occupied by pointless and fleeting content that we will likely never think of again, and it's uncomfortable but necessary to remind ourselves of this precious time we have wasted and lost forever.

Cal Newport in his book *Digital Minimalism* is explicit about this, explaining, 'As the boundary between work and life blends, jobs become more demanding, and community traditions degrade, more and more people are failing to cultivate the high-quality leisure lives that Aristotle identifies as crucial for human happiness. This leaves a void that would be near unbearable if confronted, but that can be ignored with the help of digital noise.'[9] Just like my friends, Cal recognises the imbalance, and expresses our inability to confront it head-on. We all know something is not right and we know it is making us unhealthy, but to face up to this when these digital devices have become so intrinsic to us isn't a comfortable or easy conversation. But it is an important one.

It's time we started having open conversations around how much scrolling and social media addiction is impacting and taking away from our lives. Openly admitting we spend much more time online than we'd like, rather than feeling ashamed to acknowledge this, is key to reclaiming our lives from addictive algorithms. Mikaela Loach is an activist and content creator who made the decision to take her weekends offline a few years ago as a way of setting boundaries between her personal and work life. As someone whose digital platform is fundamental to her role as a climate activist and author, she realised that after relentlessly working constantly and never switching off, it was affecting her ability to not only communicate and organise but to enjoy her life more widely.

'I realised I had developed an addiction to social media, [. . .] it was having a really negative impact on my life, never being present and never de-stressing.' For many people for whom their content has become their full-time job, stepping away can present challenges both mentally and logistically. For Mikaela, recognising that social media is simply a means to an end has allowed her to let go of guilt that previously stopped her from being able to set boundaries with her use of social media. 'Seeing social media as a tool is important. [We need to make sure] that even if social media disappeared our work could still continue, we can't rely on these platforms because these platforms were not created for social justice.'

When I think about how much content I consume online per day, the amount of content I intentionally seek out probably makes up less than 1 per cent of what I see. Before the timelines became jumbled into one endless stream of content vomit, we had to be intentional about what we sought out. This was before chronological feeds were changed to be ordered for engagement, where content that is more likely to provoke a reaction is prioritised over the most recent content. This inevitably keeps us scrolling for longer. I remember when I'd check Instagram and once I was up to date, I'd log off satisfied and carry on with my day. Back then, time on social media was a chunk *out* of my day, rather than the underlying noise that blended into it. Today my feed is littered with content I never chose to consume, but end up getting drawn into nonetheless. This is a universal experience in the digital age where consuming content has become as second nature as breathing. More and more, I've been experiencing what I now call post-scroll comedown. The best way I can describe it is a sudden wave of low mood, despair and anxiety that comes after a long scrolling session. From feeling guilty about the time I've just lost, to subconsciously comparing myself to those strangers I've engaged with on the explore page, to feeling I should be working overtime to keep up with those achieving things I admire, I am left feeling overwhelmed and deflated.

Recently, I've started to ask myself questions before or while I scroll, such as why am I doing this, what feeling is urging me to scroll at this moment? The easy and passive nature of scrolling means we often shut out our critical thinking, and I have made efforts to bring it back. It's something you could try too. When you are pulled to check on your phone, ask yourself why. Are you just bored or are you seeking out information? When you scroll aimlessly, ask yourself what you could be doing with this time, and why you aren't at this point. Ask yourself whether you like being on Instagram or whether you love photography. Do you love posting selfies or do you have a passion for beauty? Do you enjoy tweeting or are you a keen writer, or aspiring journalist? Are you obsessed with TikTok skits or are you an amateur actor or comedian in the making? Taking that same passion you commit to using these apps and channelling it into the hobbies and activities they relate to offline can make your life more fulfilling. Once you understand where your motivation to use them comes from, you can be more intentional and selective with your time, balancing the online sharing with the offline doing. This is a liberating act. Sometimes you have to get frank and harsh with yourself to make this positive shift towards logging off.

Marc Damie is an engineer and researcher in privacy-preserving technologies, specialising in building ethical digital services. As someone in the tech industry, you might not expect him to be so critical of the way our digital world currently looks, but you'd be wrong. Marc believes that whilst tech companies vitally need to change how they're working, we also need to change our own expectations of social media, and what we want from it. His experience of switching from a platform that uses addictive design features to a platform that doesn't use these toxic design features made him realise how much we've become used to addictive feeds, and how we actively have to withdraw to break the cycle of addiction.

'When I switched from Twitter (and its algorithmic feed) to Mastodon (and its chronological feed), it was so frustrating – the infinite scroll disappears. Once I had seen the new posts, I had nothing left to do . . . except disconnecting. After a few days, I got used to it and it felt really good.' With the simple and non-addictive design features of Mastodon, Marc felt in control of his time again. And his 'withdrawal' experience should prompt anyone to answer the key questions: 'What do we expect from social media? What is good social media?'

I expect most of us haven't answered these questions and instead we continually live vicariously through social media without realising that this time could be spent offline, really connecting to each other and pouring into our communities. For much of my life, I have viewed social media as my main form of community, and it's no coincidence that for young people who have grown up in the age of austerity, where youth centres have been shut down and third spaces stripped of vital public funding, we've flocked online to build the community we've been deprived of offline. On reflection of my own social media over the past ten years of my life, I've noticed in myself that I engage with digital communities far more often than I do physical ones. I know people I follow online but have never met better than I know my neighbours. I can reel off digital third spaces that I admire with ease, but ask me for somewhere to go to connect with other young people offline and I'd struggle to answer.

Social media has also allowed for the growing visibility of diverse communities. For people who have been excluded and marginalised, such as LGBTQ+ communities and Muslims, having the opportunity to connect online with like-minded people can be a safe haven. While representation often gets critiqued for its limitations, being part of a community of people who have a shared sense of identity can be a reminder you're not alone and this is essential for a sense of empowerment and belonging. But while our adoption of social media as our main means of community building can be practical and useful, it cannot replace the offline world and human connections forged in person. The continued erasure of those vital community spaces and the human connection it can bring is sapping meaning from our lives and entrenching boundaries between groups. Making our digital communities an offline reality can enhance these connections, but also open doors and avenues to other ones. Not everything is what you see online and sometimes these spaces may not actually feel right for you, yet they might in other examples. If we all were intentional about making community something that exists beyond our screens, social media might be a useful tool to connect us.

There are already many digital communities that centre interpersonal connection over digital engagement to ensure they transcend our screens and create impact on the lives they're engaging with online. Casual Readers Club is a community book club that personifies this, with their motto 'irl network because reading is communal' as strident evidence of their mission. Their events have led to meet-ups across continents, with their community rebuilding third spaces and opportunities to connect that have been dwindling in recent years. Flock Together is another community that uses social media platforms to connect to its members so they can host monthly birdwatching walks in nature for people of colour. What started with an Instagram exchange when Nadeem reached out to Ollie on Instagram to share his mutual love for birds, Ollie suggested starting a birdwatching collective. In 2020, in the context of a global lockdown and Black Lives Matter protests, Flock Together was born, a vital space to recharge and restore now with a thriving and building offline community too.

This is exactly why we must decentre social media from our lives. It is far from easy, but it's possible. Awareness is often acknowledged as the first step of change, and when it comes to our social media habits, I do believe that awareness and acceptance is key to unlearning these addictive impulses. If you truly want to live your life more offline, you must release yourself from the fear of missing out. If anything, the fact that these social media platforms have so much of a hold on us shows us that we are deeply social beings who care about how we are perceived and treated by others. We are drawn to connection and attention. But that connection shouldn't be funnelled into apps which individualise and atomise us from each other. We instead ought to channel those deep desires for connection and love towards collective goals and community building. With the growing tide of pressing issues of climate crisis, inequality and polarisation facing our species, the time to reconnect offline is now.

Sudden loss forces you to look head-on at the possibility of death and your time running out. It makes you think about what regrets you don't want to be left with. I often spend time reflecting on how my life might look different if the time I spent erratically scrolling was spent on things I love doing: spending time with my friends and family, reading books, going to talks and visiting exhibitions, immersing myself in bodies of water, pursuing new hobbies outside the digital realm. I feel certain my life would be much happier. Rather than watching someone do the things I want to do and envying them or living through them, I might have more time to make them happen for myself. When I'm near the end of my life, I doubt I'll look back and say, 'I wish I had consumed more content.' It'll likely be the opposite – I wish I had looked up at the sky instead of it through a screen; I wish I had felt that moment deeply instead of distilling it through a camera lens, I wish I had looked my friend in the eye when we had that intimate conversation.

We must reclaim our collective attention if we are to be fully present in our offline world. Doing so will enable us to tackle the issues that demand our full attention and become fully embodied in our lives. Being conscious in our use of digital devices is the first step towards reclaiming our time and our agency. Retraining our attention span to be able to concentrate on tasks that require deep flow, instead of constant task switching, is possible, but it takes intention. Picking up this book has been a great start.

CHAPTER 5

Can Anyone Be Safe Online?

'I don't have a kid, but I have a nephew that I put some boundaries on. There are some things that I won't allow; I don't want them on a social network.'

Tim Cook, CEO of Apple[1]

'Stay safe', 'take care', 'look after yourself'. From childhood, we are given these clear instructions to be aware and keep ourselves away from harm. We are taught that safety is our responsibility and something that we must take ownership of individually. Whether it's learning not to be tempted into the back of a van or car by a nefarious stranger, practising self-defence or carrying mace and rape alarms, there are seemingly endless well-intentioned measures to improve personal safety. We live in a world that fails to keep us safe and so these interventions often feel like our only option. We grew up prepared to face danger in the outside world, but then digital technology exploded on to the scene and brought potential harm into our lives in a way no one could have expected. In our pockets, handbags and bedrooms are devices that have the potential to be exceptionally dangerous or influence us to disregard safety entirely. 'Stay safe' has acquired a whole new meaning, but in a digital world ruled by addictive algorithms and Big Tech impunity, approaches that focus on individual responsibility are not enough to protect us, especially the most vulnerable in our society.

Archie Battersbee was a bright, cheeky and happy-go-lucky twelve-year-old. His mum Hollie tells me that he was a child full of energy: 'Some might say hyperactive; I would say a gift.' He tried every sport you could imagine, including football, rugby, MMA, gymnastics, all from the age of three. His passion for sports could be traced throughout their house; it had become his personal gym and his mum loved that his passion was so strong.

One weekend, Hollie and Archie went out for a bite to eat and came home with plans to go to the cinema that evening. Always playful, Archie decided to play a prank on his mum, offering Hollie some sweets from his gym bag only to reveal their pet rabbit inside. They'd burst into laughter together, and Hollie told Archie to put the rabbit away. Hollie could never have imagined that that would be the last time she would see Archie smile and hear his laugh. Just minutes later, Hollie discovered Archie unconscious on the stairs, and her whole world collapsed. She desperately performed CPR on her son with a neighbour she had called for help while they painstakingly waited for the ambulance to arrive. Archie was taken to Southend University Hospital after suffering cardiac arrest, and he was then placed in an induced coma. Archie's life support was devastatingly turned off in August 2022 after a four-month battle between his family and the hospital.

Hollie believes Archie had been taking part in the blackout challenge, a viral and dangerous TikTok phenomenon that involved people holding their breath or choking themselves using belts or bag straps to see how long they could stay conscious for, until they passed out. Archie was found with a dressing-gown cord around his neck. TikTok, the second most popular social media platform, is currently facing multiple lawsuits from parents who say their children have died from accidental strangulation whilst attempting to do the blackout challenge, which they learned how to do from the platform. This may have been as many as twenty children in eighteen months.

For example, in December 2021, ten-year-old Nylah Anderson was found lifeless in her bedroom by her mother after taking part in the same challenge, and a forensic analysis of her phone showed that she had used TikTok to watch and film a blackout challenge video before she choked.[2] In 2022, her mother, Tawainna Anderson, sued TikTok for wrongful death in the US District Court in Eastern Pennsylvania.[3] Her suit claimed that TikTok was 'programming children for the sake of corporate profits and promoting addiction', while being 'a predatory and manipulative app' that pushes 'exceedingly and unacceptably dangerous challenges'. Following her relentless fight for justice, a momentous decision was finally made in 2024 by Judge Paul Matey, ruling that the app is not protected by Section 230 of the Communications Decency Act, which protects internet platforms like X, TikTok and YouTube from being held liable for content posted by third-party users.[4]

What happened to Archie and Nylah could have happened to anyone, and the blackout challenge is just one of many viral acts on social media platforms. Since the 2010s, viral challenges have exploded on the apps: examples include the ice bucket challenge, the Don't Rush challenge, the cinnamon challenge, the salt and ice challenge and the Harlem Shake. Not all of these challenges are dangerous, and many are fun. I remember taking part in the Harlem Shake in Year 9 with my whole class, and it just involved a funny dance that we could then post on Facebook. But so many we see online today are unsafe and involve taking risks that we would never encourage taking offline. I remember doing the cinnamon challenge, which involves eating a large spoonful of cinnamon, in my back garden, with two school friends sitting in front of their phones documenting every second. As soon as I put the spoon in my mouth, my body filled with panic that I was going to die as I started to choke on the dry mound of dust. Often these challenges seem like nothing but a bit of innocent fun, and for many, they are. Some have raised millions for charity, some purely offered us a sense of connection and global community especially during the global pandemic. For example, when the Don't Rush challenge went viral during the Covid-19 pandemic, it brought a rare moment of joy. It was a challenge that involved a before and after glam transformation in sync with the song 'Don't Rush' and it was clear that people were happy to have an excuse to do their make-up and feel good at a time when this was, for the most part, a rarity.

However, viral challenges spread at unstoppable speeds, and social media platforms fail (and are reluctant) to prevent their circulation because viral content means big business. This can lead to dire consequences, especially when the challenges promote risky behaviour. People jump on to these challenges, lulled into a false sense of security by the broad reach and novelty of them, and then when things go wrong, the individuals and their families have to pick up the pieces. An inquest ruled in 2024 that Archie died after doing a 'prank or experiment gone wrong', most likely the viral blackout challenge, though a coroner said there was no evidence for this. Despite the likelihood that he was partaking in a social media challenge, his mother Hollie cannot get answers from TikTok, the app he was using just hours before he was found unconscious. Despite her endless battle with the social media platform and the police investigating Archie's death, she cannot see the video Archie watched, vital information which could give her the answers as to why he died. With Nylah the connection was explicit, but social media companies still plead innocence rather than take accountability.

Until Nylah's case, companies like Google, Instagram and TikTok had largely completely evaded any responsibility for the harmful content that is hosted on their platforms, even when users have lost their lives as a result. This is because of the archaic laws that apply to social media platforms. The most important law you need to know in order to understand the impunity that tech companies are granted is Section 230 of the Communications Decency Act. A US law born in the internet's infancy and drafted before social media even existed, this piece of legislation was introduced as a way of protecting online platforms from defamation cases for the content that users posted on them. But this loophole of unaccountability has set a precedent for an internet that is a Wild West of harmful and hateful content. Since the founding fathers of the internet are not considered 'publishers' of content, they aren't held directly responsible for the consequences of that content. As victims' rights lawyer Carrie Goldberg writes, 'A narrow law created in 1996 intended to shield burgeoning internet service providers from defamation lawsuits – Section 230 of the Communications Decency Act – has been Big Tech's get-out-of-court-free card.'[5]

Since the public backlash that has been triggered following cases like Archie's and Nylah's, TikTok has made a feeble attempt to demonstrate its commitments to 'community wellbeing'. If you were to search for the #BlackoutChallenge, you would now be signposted to the Samaritans helpline. Directing users who are in need to support services is vital, but this intervention was only an indication of how TikTok didn't understand its users at all. Children who joined in on these challenges weren't suicidal, they were taking part in something that was being promoted on the platform as innocent fun. But for TikTok, a platform known for these types of trending challenges, moderating them properly is its last resort. As Mitchell Clark, tech writer for The Verge writes, 'Challenges are a core part of the TikTok experience, to the point where competitors have started trying to integrate them into their platforms in an attempt at appealing to TikTok users.'[6] TikTok's failure to adopt a prevention over cure approach – and clamp down on dangerous challenges – means that young users continue to be at risk of these types of social media trends.

Challenges are not the only type of online content that can be unsafe or harmful. In the UK, we now consume more than six hours of digital media a day and such excessive exposure leaves us at risk of falling into dangerous spaces online.[7] If you've ever consciously taken time offline or attempted to reduce your daily screen time, it's likely because you've noticed that the sheer amount of content we consume is not only overwhelming for our attention span, but significantly shapes our moods and emotions too. We often think of online content as a harmless distraction. But this is far from the truth.

As we learned earlier, the algorithms that endlessly drip-feed us digital content are hard-wired to track our online behaviours and predict our emotional responses, to keep us logged on at whatever cost. Algorithms do not decipher what content is healthy or harmful, which means that so much of what we see online is not fit for human consumption. Research by Amnesty International found that it took just one hour for TikTok's algorithm to show dummy accounts that romanticise self-harm and suicide.[8]

Young people are being exposed to a whole host of toxic content. To make matters worse, research shows that we are three times more likely to click on negative content over positive content, with social media algorithms designed to maximise this effect, known as negativity bias.[9] It is the new norm that we can go from seeing a friend's euphoric engagement announcement photo to an image of inhumane violence on our feeds in a matter of milliseconds.

The algorithms that social media platforms use open up portals and gateways to other worlds we didn't know existed and immerse us in spaces that don't exist offline. They lead us down dark roads that are impossible to turn back from. Their elaborate and calculated design reels us in and keeps us online, whatever the cost, and this is what makes it extremely easy to get drawn into the darker and more dangerous sides of the internet. All it takes is a matter of seconds and if you are vulnerable, lonely or susceptible, the worlds you are introduced to can feel like a lifeboat or solace. As one eighteen-year-old student from the Philippines tells Amnesty, 'When I watch a sad video that I could relate to, suddenly my whole "For You" Page is sad and I'm in "Sadtok".'[10] Because algorithms track our behaviour, the things that make us pause, tap and catch our intrigue become digital indicators of what we will likely consume more of, meaning that algorithms are wired to expose us to content that can destabilise us. All children are curious, and naturally they are likely to click on content that they've never seen before, and this is currently creating a crisis of preventable harm for young users online.

Rachel Coldicutt OBE is a researcher and strategist specialising in the social impact of emerging technologies and the founder of Careful Industries. She described the difference between offline and online safety as being the difference between crossing the road outside your front door and crossing the motorway. 'Online everything is sped up. With the existing issue of algorithmic intensification, someone who is having a mental health crisis is going to be pushed towards harm, rather than prevented from going down that path in the first place.' Younger people are more at risk from this process. Psychologists have found that teens are more susceptible to the addictive nature of algorithms due to the prefrontal cortex – the part of the brain responsible for decision-making, judgement and impulse control – not yet being fully developed.[11]

Speak to any young person about their experiences online and I guarantee you will hear that they have seen content you would never dream of exposing a child to. Research by Ofcom in 2024 found that every single British child who was interviewed had seen violent material on the internet.[12] Harmful online content is so pervasive, it's become almost unavoidable. How can we expect any young person to thrive when this is what they're up against? 'The tech exceptionalism that has allowed global companies to export hate, discord, violence and exposure alongside their products has made for a world in which millions of children suffer. [. . .] The opportunity cost of this is seen in the bodies and lived experience of children,' says Baroness Beeban Kidron, a member of the House of Lords and the founder of 5Rights. Seeing such content triggers unnatural reactions that they would only have if experiencing things in real life. The brain cannot differentiate real threat and threat played out in a two-minute video, and the body will react accordingly. We don't know the long-term impact of seeing such content on our brains, but research so far suggests that our digital sphere is anything but good for us, and children are the most at risk.

It is a deep injustice that children's safety and wellbeing is being compromised whilst social media companies make their billions. As Ian Russell rightly says, social media platforms are 'monetising misery', and the culture of impunity has got to end. The self-regulation that tech companies have so far been entrusted with does not work and although government regulation doesn't fix things overnight, it does give us a safety net to prevent harms, and an accountability framework for when incidents do happen. The corporate negligence we see from social media giants is fuelling the mental health crisis facing our young people and is knowingly depriving them of the right to live a safe and happy life.

In 2017, Ian's family was touched by the real-life impacts of insidious algorithms that prey on our vulnerabilities and keep us scrolling whatever the cost, when his fourteen-year-old daughter, Molly, lost her life. Molly Russell was a positive and bright young teenager. She loved horse riding, she had recently played the lead role in her school play and was obsessed with the band 5 Seconds of Summer. In the last year of her life, she became more withdrawn and spent more time in her room, something that many parents of teenagers will have witnessed as puberty descends and they navigate this emotionally intense phase of growing up. But Molly was getting sucked into a place she couldn't escape from through the devices she was using. She found herself consuming content recommended to her on Instagram and Pinterest that was all about self-harm, suicide, depression and anxiety. It is now known that she had seen at least 2,100 Instagram posts related to depression, self-harm and suicide in the last six months of her life.[13]

One fateful day, Molly could no longer cope and took the decision to end her life. This content she had been exposed to prior to her death was so harmful and traumatic that a consultant child psychologist told the inquest he couldn't sleep for a week after seeing certain posts Molly had seen. The same content this coroner found 'almost impossible to watch' was deemed 'safe' by Meta's standards, according to the company's head of health and wellbeing Elizabeth Lagone.[14] In a historic inquest in September 2022, senior coroner Andrew

Walker concluded that 'Molly Rose Russell died from an act of self-harm whilst suffering from depression and the negative effects of online content.'[15] The inquest ruling opened the floodgates to a realisation that had not before been acknowledged: online content is not simply a flimsy distraction from day-to-day life but a force that shapes the way we think, influences how we behave and in the worst circumstances can cause us death. Social media platforms have not been designed to be safe, but instead have been designed to consume us and engulf us whole. At any time for any one of us, the timeline could quickly become an echo chamber of despair.

No one should be shown content that promotes suicide, and if this were to happen on a billboard in a public place, there would be widespread outrage. Why should social media platforms be any different? Are they not a public space like any other? We are in the midst of a crisis in young people's mental health, yet social media companies are cashing in. More and more whistle-blowers are coming forward to express their concerns about the algorithms that determine our digital diet and shape our lives. In 2020, Charles Bahr, a former TikTok ad sales manager, warned his superiors that he was being shown content promoting suicide and self-harm on the app, with him being reduced to tears at what he was seeing. He suggested that instead of censoring content from users who were struggling, the app should instead boost positive and uplifting content.[16] Months later, he was fired. Not long after, company documents leaked in 2021 by Facebook whistle-blower and data scientist Frances Haugen revealed that Meta knew its products were harming children.

This wasn't enough to change things, for in 2024, leading psychologist Lotte Rubæk, who advised Meta on suicide prevention and self-harm, quit her role, accusing the tech giant of 'turning a blind eye' to harmful content and repeatedly ignoring expert advice.[17] Tech companies themselves push back against online safety legislation that aims to tackle harmful and dangerous content, arguing that this type of regulation would impose on freedom of speech by cranking down on what can be said and circulated online. These claims fail to recognise that the most important human right – the right to life – is being put at risk daily by the failure to tackle harmful content. Their products are fundamentally unsafe, and this is taking precious lives. Adopting a human rights lens to social media and digital technologies would empower us to strike the essential balance that is required for us to protect free speech while ensuring safety for all. Online safety is not a choice, it is a fundamental right we all deserve.

Undoubtedly, parents are feeling the growing burden of keeping their children safe in a digital world they have next to no control over. They're told to regularly have conversations with their children about their smartphone use, place limits on their screen time and even ban devices at home. But the duty of care for online safety doesn't fall solely with parents, it falls with tech companies. Parents are not responsible for regulating or moderating the content we see on social media, and most parents never see what their children are exposed to online because of the online bubbles that algorithms divide us into. As Zara, a mother of two girls of primary school age shared with me, 'I often think how I'm going to protect them from that evil and will I even be able to?'

When the impacts of social media are so pervasive and potentially dangerous, it's easy to resort to smartphone bans as a short-term solution. As another parent asks me, 'If you have an electric saw, you keep it locked in the cupboard in the garage, but how can we do that with social media?' Banning social media and smartphones can feel like a quick fix to an overwhelming problem, and one that many understandably anxious parents feel the need to turn to. But a smartphone ban without holding social media companies to account would be the equivalent of sticking a plaster on a gaping wound. This can also backfire and make vulnerable young people more at risk, by alienating children from their parents, breaking down communication and eroding trust. Smartphone bans deflect the responsibility of safety away from the creators of these products and place the burden on us once again.

Instead, we need to tackle the problem at the root and tech companies have to be forced to act. Regulation to make algorithms safe by design, by deciphering between harmful and helpful content, would help to keep us safe online. Design It For Us is a youth-led coalition fighting to make this happen. They advocate for a safer digital world and pressure decision-makers to hold social media platforms to account through legislation and policy. Its team members – many of whom are students – have committed to applying pressure on key decision-makers to make social media platforms safe, revealing how young people recognise the stakes of this just as much as parents. This is the bare minimum if we want to build a digital world that is healthy and beneficial for all of us and the future generations.

While I've focused on the experiences of children in this chapter, online safety is not just essential for children, it's essential for all of us. We all live on a mental health spectrum that we are constantly moving along. Any one of us can become vulnerable to experiencing poor mental health at any time in our lives, because just like our physical health, our mental health is constantly being affected by factors beyond our control. And the same way mental health does not age-discriminate, harmful online content doesn't either. 'You don't stop having suicidal feelings or self-harming as soon as you turn eighteen and this new law must help protect everyone, on any site, whether they are sixteen or sixty-six. [. . .] With every day that passes without action, we lose an opportunity to save lives,' says Mubeen Bhutta, head of policy, public affairs and campaigns at Samaritans. This is what makes online safety both a collective and urgent fight.

'Move fast and break things' goes Mark Zuckerberg's famous slogan. It speaks to the ideology of relentless technological innovation, but at what human cost? We can all agree that a world where children are being encouraged to take their lives, or film themselves doing life-threatening 'challenges' is not innovative. Real innovation would mean that our lives are enhanced and empowered by the digital technologies that we use. As Baroness Beeban Kidron says, 'The infinite possibilities that technology brings are worthless if they also bring pain and harm to children and young people.' Currently, tech is certainly moving fast and breaking things, but the things being broken are not replaceable. Social media companies can no longer be depended on to change their ways voluntarily, and their CEOs cannot be trusted to act out of the kindness of their hearts, because up until now they have failed to show their humanity. Unless these companies lose out financially, whether this is through imposed fines, consumer boycotts or their market values dropping, they will continue business as usual. The tech industry can no longer rule itself, because for as long as it does we will all lose out.

CHAPTER 6

What's Angry, Divisive and Spreads Fake News?

'The enemy is out there – just check your feed.'
Tobias Rose-Stockwell, author of *Outrage Machine*[1]

'Our recommendation systems grow the problem.'
Meta Report, 2016[2]

Professor Meareg was a pioneering figure. As one of just three qualified professors in Ethiopia, he made a respectable career for himself as a lecturer in analytical chemistry. He was not simply a well-respected intellectual, however. A champion of young people, he dedicated his life to getting young people into STEM subjects. He was the author of chemistry textbooks for secondary school students, taught at every level of higher education and had published over forty-seven scientific articles. In 2022 and 2023, he was invited to present his findings at nineteen international scientific conferences across the globe, with the impacts of his research spanning continents. Reading his biography, it's easy to feel out of your depth, but Professor Meareg was a humble and kind soul, whose tireless dedication to his community earned him a lifelong legacy.

But one day, the life and legacy of Meareg was cut saddeningly short. On 10 October 2021, his life was changed forever when he saw a post on a Facebook page that falsely accused him of a horrendous crime. The unfolding civil war in Ethiopia had subjected many Tigrayan professionals and community leaders like him to smear campaigns in an attempt to breed ethnic violence and sow the seeds of division. Overnight, Professor Meareg became a target and the inflammatory post started to gain attention, and quickly. What followed was a relentless doxxing campaign on Facebook, with strangers leaking Professor Meareg's personal details and home address, with comments calling for people to take justice into their own hands. Fearing for his father's life, his son Abrham reported the misinformation to Facebook, but to no avail. The company failed to respond to Abrham, let alone remove the posts. Abrham's worries didn't subside, but he hoped the anger would dissipate and the timeline would move on as it does. But weeks later, Professor Meareg was walking home when a mob of militants ambushed him in the street, chanting the very comments that had made up the Facebook posts. He was shot, and they left him to bleed out on the street for seven agonising hours before he died.

What happened to Professor Meareg may sound like a freak incident, a heated moment of unexplainable violence, but the reality is that this collective outrage is something all social media platforms tap into. The increasingly polarised nature of our online world that has come as a result of outrage-inducing social media architecture, designed to keep us logged on. How many times have you found yourself getting sucked into a heated debate on X, on a matter that you're not even that interested in? I've had countless experiences of wasted moments lost to the timeline, trying to catch up on a trail of drama that in reality, I don't care about. I've also fallen victim to the temptation of responding to trolls, and have often got drawn into a cycle of catty comebacks that get us nowhere except a short-lived kick and ego boost. This is a collective experience that many of us have lived online, and it's due to the mechanics of our platforms that we get sucked into doing so. In a business model where user engagement is the goal, outrage is an immensely powerful tool online, and one that social media companies leverage in order to keep us logged in.

Facebook's own data has shown that borderline content – defined as content that is almost at the threshold for being too graphic, misleading or offensive – attracts much higher engagement than more neutral posts.[3] One study found that Twitter users who received more likes and retweets when they expressed outrage were more likely to express outrage in their posts again.[4] Just adding emotionally charged words can determine the performance of your posts, so it's no wonder we feel inclined to do so, often without even realising. As author Naomi Klein explores in *Doppelganger*, in the attention economy where digital engagement and clicks can translate into monetisation, people are actively incentivised by tech elites and their platforms' algorithms to post the most inflammatory and outrageous content possible. In 2021, this was revealed publicly when Meta whistle-blower Frances Haugen explained that leaders of social media firms actively choose algorithms that fuel division, as a way of keeping us online.[5] Mix emotive posts with politics and you have a toxic concoction, and a potent breeding ground for radicalisation and extremist action. Research found that each negative word about political opponents increases the odds of a social media post being shared by 67 per cent.[6] And so, this process doesn't just keep us passively online, it incentivises us to keep the flames of polarisation burning. In places where division and hatred are already brewing, social media algorithms prey on this and stir up chaos.

A historical moment that made visible the potency that online anger and political polarisation has offline was the storming of the Capitol Building in Washington DC in 2021. Across the world, many of us watched, captivated, as a mob of far-right extremists stormed the home of American democracy. These extremists were members of the Proud Boy movement made up of neo-Nazis, white supremacists and the conspiracy group QAnon, and on 6 January they climbed walls bearing weapons, enraged following Donald Trump's election defeat. Never in American history had a president been charged with a plot to overturn a democratic election result before this moment. But while these events saw a coming together of far-right actors in real life, there was something that had triggered the events that came about that day in the digital sphere. A single tweet, ending with the words 'Be there, be wild!' from the former president himself was an invitation and an incitement. This right-wing mobilisation, which led to several deaths and hundreds of arrests, revealed the potency of emotional outrage online and what it means for our lives offline.

Donald Trump is a prime example of someone who has consistently capitalised on the emotive charge of his tweets, tapping into what Tobias Rose-Stockwell terms the 'outrage machine' and its potential to fan the flames of political movements. On Instagram, the account most often reported for inciting violence was Donald Trump's official account.[7] The former president would tweet directly to his supporters, knowing that they would flock to defend him. In September 2020, for example, ahead of a debate, he tweeted urging members of the violent far-right group Proud Boys to 'stand back and stand by'. Then, two days after the storming of the Capitol, Twitter finally banned him due to 'risk of further incitement of violence'.[8] When asked why the company did not moderate the former president's tweets or suspend him before the chaos that unfolded at the Capitol, one Twitter employee said that they believed 'Twitter relished in the knowledge that they were also the favourite and most used service of the former president.'[9] It's unsurprising that a company that profits from traffic would be keen to continue to host controversial figures, whose content can attract huge swathes of outrage and disgrace, as well as amplification from fans and trolls alike. It's also no wonder that serial entrepreneur Elon Musk then took the decision to sack a third of Twitter's global trust and safety staff,[10] when hosting harmful and divisive content is something the platform profits from, or even becomes known for.

The loss of Professor Meareg was not only devastating for his family but it also forced them to flee their home country to protect their physical safety, and they are now refugees in America. 'The void left by his departure is felt deeply, and the pain is magnified by the knowledge that he was taken from us in such a senseless and brutal manner,' his son Abrham told me. Not only did this loss impact them physically, but it has scarred them spiritually, with many of Meareg's family members questioning their faith. How could a person as hard-working, humble and kind as Professor Meareg be torn away from his life and family in such a senseless and violent act? This traumatic loss could have been totally avoided with proper regulation of false information and the simple action of removing the post, and instead his family must face the repercussions. 'We have lost our priceless father . . . they erased our best childhood memories, they have stolen our dreams and aspirations,' said Abrham. Corporations are failing to tackle misinformation and disinformation, and this has consequences that unfold beyond the feed. Abrham tells me that he holds Facebook accountable for his father's murder, and he is now fighting for justice through a legal case against Facebook.

This is a global issue. In 2017, the UN accused Facebook of allowing its platform to provoke the genocide in Myanmar, which was responsible for the displacement of over 700,000 Rohingya Muslims, and resulted in the torture, killing and rape of Rohingya people. Similarly, Amnesty International found that leading up to the escalation of the military violence against the Rohingya, Facebook in Myanmar became an echo chamber of anti-Rohingya content. Global Witness submitted ads including hate speech inciting violence and genocide, and disinformation in Myanmar, Ethiopia, Kenya, Brazil and Norway and Meta did not reject a single ad for publication.[11] This mirrors a pattern of complicity from Meta in allowing misinformation to spread and exacerbate atrocities, as seen in Myanmar, Sri Lanka, Indonesia and Cambodia. Big Tech companies cash in on chaos, whilst societies suffer the consequences and lasting impacts of online outrage. To add insult to injury, in some countries, social media companies don't even attempt to keep users safe from harmful content. Evidence from the internal Facebook files leaked by Haugen in 2021 revealed the platform spends 87 per cent of its budget for tackling misinformation on English language content, despite the fact that only 9 per cent of its users are English-speaking.[12] Staggeringly, some languages still do not even have a single content moderator dedicated to them by platforms, leaving gaps for hate speech, misinformation, violence and abuse to blossom.[13]

Since the algorithms that make up our feeds show us content that we are more likely to interact with, it often means the content falls into one of two extreme categories – posts we already agree with or posts we definitely don't. Content that makes us feel more extreme emotions is more likely to draw us in, hook, line and sinker. This is why misinformation that promotes religious and racial hatred is so potent online, because of the emotional outrage that it invokes in users, because these are things we care about so deeply. In the UK, we saw this within our own communities in 2024, when far-right riots spread following the circulation of racist and Islamophobic misinformation online after three girls were stabbed and killed by a man in Southport. The active spread and weaponisation of false claims by far-right figures with huge online clout and the failure of social media platforms to clamp down on it paved the way for offline violence. Social media platforms cash in on this growing extremism and hatred we see today. Research by Facebook found that 64 per cent of people who join extremist groups on Facebook are doing so because Facebook's algorithms sent them there.[14] As Matthew Feldman, expert in far-right extremism says, 'It is difficult to think of a much better example of online harms breaching the real world than a fake story demonising Muslims and people of colour and leading to riots on the streets.'[15]

There are parallels between the far-right riots in the UK and the brutal murder of Abrham's father. In both cases, social media platforms played a part in allowing misinformation and hatred to gain traction and failed to intervene. In our vastly unregulated online territory, disinformation and misinformation – or what you might know as fake news – spreads like wildfire. This isn't just down to trigger-happy users retweeting without caution, it's down to platform design. A study by the Integrity Institute found that misinformation on X had thirty-five times more reach than truthful information.[16] The severity of this cannot be underestimated. Misinformation and disinformation aren't just dodgy clickbait headlines, they are toxic smear campaigns against activists, leaked falsified rumours that shame public figures and deepfake hoaxes that try to sway voters. If the growing epidemic of false information is known to be so harmful yet the solution is so simple, why are platforms failing to act? Sadly, content that is false is extremely engaging. In 2018, research done at MIT found that fake news is 70 per cent more likely to be retweeted than true news stories, and it takes true stories six times longer to reach 1,500 people.[17] Similarly, an Oxford research study of 22 million tweets showed that Twitter users had shared more 'misinformation, polarising, and conspiratorial content' than had shared actual news stories.[18]

To avoid being forced to tackle misinformation at the root – real action that would require them to challenge their own business model – social media platforms adopt smokescreen policies that simply perform an attempt to do so. When discussing many of the anti-mis/disinformation initiatives that platforms have adopted in recent years, Sam Doak, senior fact checker at Logically Facts, tells me that many of these are tokenistic. 'They want to do the bare minimum to avoid regulation.' To paint a picture of how tech companies fail when left to their own devices to self-regulate, simply look at the case of Myanmar, where there were only four Burmese speakers at Facebook to monitor its 7.3 million Burmese users.[19] A *Guardian* investigation into TikTok found that the platform failed to follow their own policies on content moderation, with content moderators being told not to apply their removal policies to high-profile figures. Internal communications from the company revealed that content made by top creators that would be deemed 'edge cases' – content which verges on breaking TikTok guidelines – was to be treated with more leniency than normal creators.[20] What this means is content that verges on being unsafe, fake news or misinformation, hateful or abusive, is enabled to spread by the platform. So far, much of Big Tech's dedication to regulating misinformation has been fake promises and empty words.

Misinformation is one element, but social media platforms have also come to offer taboo and extreme conversations a safe home, fuelling their dispersion and breeding confusion. Figures like Andrew Tate, Tommy Robinson and Jordan Peterson are platformed for their hot takes and 'controversial' theories. Harmful and divisive ideologies such as Holocaust denial and climate change denial spread on social media platforms and are influencing people the world over with dangerous theories and ideologies. Over the past century, we have made huge strides to stamp out bigotry and discrimination from our institutions, our attitudes, our worldviews. We publicly call out prejudice that was deemed the norm just a few decades ago. In the meantime, these communities and their harmful beliefs have found a new home online and any of the positive advancements in building tolerance and solidarity has been set ablaze.

These figures and their theories are also not being interrogated and false information is not being identified as such, because of confirmation bias. 'It's not a very common thing for people to see a narrative that confirms their worldview and then go through the process of scrutinising it,' says Sam Doak. I'm guilty of this. Even as a journalist who takes great pride in seeking and upholding the truth, I myself have fallen victim to the psychological forces that our social media platforms tap into. In 2024, at a time when Starbucks was the target of consumer boycotts in solidarity with Palestine, a screenshot of a watermelon mug they had listed on their website was shared on X. The watermelon had become symbolic of Palestinian liberation, which led people to accuse Starbucks of selling the mug to win back customers. I quickly tweeted, slamming Starbucks for their icky performative action. But soon after going viral, fact checkers from established media outlets found that the product was not new, it was stock from before the conflict escalated in October 2023.[21] The pressure we have internalised to constantly speak up online in fear of being seen as not caring or ignorant of an issue fuels the spread of misinformation. There is so much noise and pressure to be ever-vocal online that we rarely take the time to critically listen or think before we post. Before checking the facts, we rush to join others who are demonstrating outrage. We're all susceptible to becoming a secondary spreader of misinformation and contributing to the snowball effect. Just like those chain messages on early Facebook feeds that stated 'share or ten years' bad luck!', we are incentivised to share nonsense without even thinking about it twice.

As more of us come to use social media as our main way of keeping up to date with news and the issues we care about, the failure to prevent misinformation and disinformation puts democracy at risk. Artificial intelligence is also creating new opportunities for false information to spread, seeping into our networks, weaving its way into the background noise of our digital landscape, undetected. Research by Algorithm Watch found that Bing Chat, the AI chatbot on Microsoft's search engine, makes up false scandals about politicians and provides wrong polling numbers, with a third of answers containing factual errors.[22] Whilst catfishing was once a targeted and laborious effort, bad actors can now spread false information at the click of a button. In 2024, potential Democrat voters in America were the targets of an insidious attack on their right to vote; a deepfake robocall of Joe Biden was circulated where the voice discouraged voters to vote in primary elections. This is unfolding across all chasms of the political spectrum, and it will impact all of us.

If you feel as though you live in a perpetual state of confusion, overwhelm and content burnout, exposure to misinformation online is likely one of the causes. You might suspect that you would be able to decipher between what's real and what's not, but the fact is that misleading information now makes up the background of our digital lives; it is a constant hum that we've become desensitised to. If you've seen the Pope in a puffer jacket, or a collection of Tory MPs doing manual labour jobs, you've already fallen victim to a more detectable example of disinformation. It's easy to fall for these images because as we scroll our timelines, we rarely give a second thought to the content we see.

Social media doesn't ask us to be critical thinkers – the way its algorithms work boost hot topics and trend-based conversations which make us feel that we don't have the time to do our research because of fear we'll miss out on being included in the conversation. Many of us saw this live in action in 2022 when a post about Iran claiming that 15,000 protesters were sentenced to death went viral.[23] Garnering over 315,000 likes in two days and shares from public figures including Justin Trudeau, Viola Davis and Sophie Turner, the post had tapped into people's fears of infringements on democracy and our right to protest. But the 'news' was false; Iran was doing no such thing. While our timelines come to replace traditional media as our main sources of information, critical thinking is a skill that is more important than ever.

The fact that platforms aren't classified as publishers of content means platforms aren't deemed liable for harmful content hosted on them, which is a glaring accountability loophole that urgently needs to change. If media outlets were to sell fake news, they would be legally and financially punished; similarly, if a publisher were to publish defamatory content, they would face legal action. We have existing examples of businesses held to account and the negative impact that content they share can have, and this needs to apply to Big Tech too. Imposing financial penalties on social media companies when they fail to remove misinformation and disinformation might be the only trigger that motivates them to act in the interests of user safety. Communities who have felt the lasting impacts of misinformation are already demanding this. In Myanmar, a group of Rohingya youth have called for Meta to provide a $1 million education project in the refugee camp in Cox's Bazar in Bangladesh as a way of remedying the harms of its failure to remove harmful and hateful content relating to Rohingya people. This is the least that Facebook could do as a means of digital reparations for the damage they've enabled to unfold against the Rohingya community.

It's time that we end the toxic outrage cycle that defines our digital world, instead of resigning to the false idea that despair and polarisation and division are simply facts of human nature. Altering the design of social media feeds in a way that gives users agency over what they see could make a real difference.[24] Giving users the tools to customise their feed to what they want to see rather than what algorithms determine would allow us to have more control over what content we consume, and what we feel as a result. But this still may not go far enough, especially for children.

While top-down action is what I want to demand in this book, I also know that transformation can happen at the level of the individual too. One of the most polarising phenomenons that divides us daily and prevents us from finding our common ground is cancel culture. Far from the idea spouted by far-right figures that cancel culture is some type of leftist political movement, cancel culture isn't a political issue but is symptomatic of our digital culture. The same algorithms that fuel ethnic violence, the spread of misinformation and hate speech are the ones fuelling cancel culture. This phenomenon has emerged from the algorithmic design of social media platforms which capitalise on engagement by any means, and when outrage is a fast-track route to going viral, cancel culture can touch any of us. Speaking on *Woman's Hour* about her experiences of social media pile-ons, actor and activist Jameela Jamil shares how cancel culture has become something celebrated and championed in online political spaces over the years. 'We want to own someone else; we want to humiliate someone else, and that's what generates the clicks and the claps.'[25] In the process, content sparking outrage triggered greater engagement, which has meant that even conversations around someone getting cancelled are bound to blow up.

In the process, cancel culture has meant that what were once opportunities for bridging gaps in our knowledge and progressing together have now become opportunities to label and judge each other at first glance, or worse, punish. Algorithms that are designed to addict us do not make space for error or in-betweens. As Naomi Klein writes, the polarising nature of social media has left 'binaries where thinking once lived'.[26] The destruction of the middle ground is eradicating our potential to connect across backgrounds, cultures, perspectives and more. We are losing the art of the slow burn of debate, the spontaneity of real-life human reactions and the changing of people's minds. There is less room for mistakes to be made and learned from, for people to develop their character and to change. Instead, there are only clicks and the dopamine rush of silencing the person you disagree with.

This is not to undermine the impact that harmful narratives can have, or to say that free speech ought to equate to unaccountability. Instead, we have to acknowledge that humans are messy creatures, who need to be wrong in order to learn and grow, and cancel culture doesn't account for that. The type of mob mentality we see today online is a symptom of a society that is becoming ruled by algorithms that demand our attention and push us towards extremes. Whilst social media platforms have undeniably offered us a new medium through which to share and navigate our own beliefs, worldviews and politics, their architecture has fuelled feelings of outrage, isolation and despair. The same design features that push us towards harmful content also tear us away from one another, fuelling division and eroding our sense of a shared humanity. This type of 'social' media leaves us on a weak footing for the long-term action needed to tackle the issues of our lifetime and beyond.

The solution? Slowing down and pausing before we jump to react. Jameela Jamil believes that being able to admit that you were wrong and being willing to learn and grow is the antidote to this pile-on culture that is so pervasive online, particularly on X. 'Your opinion and your identity have become so deeply intertwined, that now when someone criticises your opinion you feel as though they're attacking your entire identity and that's not the case. [. . .] We take everything so personally we don't know how to handle rejection and I think that we have become terrified of rejection, terrified of being told that we're wrong.'[27]

Cancel culture is one indication of how our individualistic culture online has become all-pervasive. In our now hypervisual economy, the individual is everything. The culture of idol worship that has emerged out of social media has meant people have come to depend and fixate on their perceived ideas of those they follow, which only risks projecting our own perceptions and expectations on to others. When those people fail to live up to our extreme expectations, we can feel betrayed, rejected, left behind. Influencers and individuals get denounced, subject to greater public scrutiny than politicians ever receive. Instead of cancelling we ought to critique, and instead of silencing we ought to debate.

Something I've come to learn in·my years of being online, witnessing movements and learning about societal issues I had never known about before, is that the learning takes time. There is beauty in being able to learn about something, take the time away to go and think deeply about it. My mum told me that during her time as a student in Istanbul, she would attend socialist meetings with anarchists who would discuss Marxist theory at length for hours. She would often have no existing knowledge about these subjects but she was curious, and with her background as the only daughter of olive farmers and the only girl in her family to go to university, she knew she could be an advocate for working-class people, and women's rights and autonomy. Between sessions, she would go away and read. 'I didn't have a clue what they were talking about half the time, but I would learn in time what I believed,' she told me.

This is the beauty of learning over time and interacting deeply with a subject. You can dig deep to understand it and from that build your own views and develop your own perspective. This is something that is often absent from social media culture and discourse. The constant and ever-changing trending topics mislead us into thinking we must constantly have the strongest opinions on whatever is most current, even if it is something we do not completely understand. The same way that our economic model of capitalism prioritises constant economic growth at any means and values this as the only indicator of societal progress, online, timely and public engagement with whatever's on the agenda today is all that matters. It fuels a shallow and ever-fleeting engagement with deeply important issues. It prevents us from asking ourselves what we can do in the long term, because we've done the posting and there will be something else that demands our attention tomorrow.

Of course, to exist in a state of constantly switching our attention between different issues does a disservice to ourselves, but also the collective. If none of us give the time to explore and advocate for something consistently for days, weeks, months, years on end, we risk missing out on the hard-won longer-term wins that come from campaigning, organising, coalition building and creating from the ground up over years, or even decades. Instead, if each of us tried to master one social issue we care deeply about, we could share that knowledge with others and work collectively to make change, instead of constantly feeling overwhelmed by how much demands our attention and how thinly we are spread.

We are emotional beings, which is why outrage has such a pull, but that means that feelings like empathy and community can have impact in equal measure, if we cultivate our online spaces to foster those over the divisive tactics of attention-seeking algorithms. Sadly, we have become used to consuming digital content at an immense pace, in a digital ecosystem where the stream never runs dry. We simply do not have the time to fact-check every single thing we see, but we can try to get wise to the mindless scrolling. As a journalist who has been reporting on digital harms and social inequality, I've often felt disappointed when I share a story I've worked on, such as how creative workers' livelihoods are being disempowered by generative AI, and it gets minimal engagement online. As the online world becomes oversaturated with content, we are being drawn to extremes that grab our attention in an instant, rather than feeling we are able to be selective in our intake. Slowing down our digital consumption can help us avoid believing everything we see online. Getting your information from credible sources, rather than strangers (or celebrities) on the internet, might seem self-explanatory, but it's easy to forget the importance of this in an age where we're being driven to extremes. Today, being on social media is a recipe for extreme emotions at extreme speeds, but it's up to us to slow down and step back.

CHAPTER 7

Body Goals

'Today, I am more familiar with many friends' and acquaintances' photos than I am with their actual faces.'
Emma Dabiri, *Disobedient Bodies*[1]

Our attention is a commodity, but it isn't our only one. Our faces, bodies and aesthetics are the hottest property in the digital sphere, and it is fracturing our sense of self and the relationship we have with our bodies on an unprecedented scale. Social media platforms expose us to unattainable beauty standards and profit from the toxic cycle of endless comparison. At the same time, their addictive algorithms push content that promotes an unhealthy relationship with our bodies to those who are most at risk of falling down the rabbit hole of no return. This isn't anything new. The commodification of beauty in the digital sphere has been around since before the internet's inception, but with aspirational imagery at your fingertips, it has taken on a whole new meaning.

From the ages of fourteen to seventeen, I'd rush home from school or college, race up to my attic bedroom, refresh my hair and top up my concealer and lip gloss, change into some variation of leggings and a crop top, and pull out my phone and take selfies until I was satisfied that one was good enough to share on Instagram. This was my daily routine for three years, when Instagram was still largely new, and it was undeniably the IT girl of social media apps. I would spend around an hour taking photos that looked essentially identical, clenching my stomach and contorting my hips to appear as small as possible. Some of my most vivid teenage memories are the numerous takes and hours I'd spend trying to get the right selfie; I wish I had spent more time chatting with my friends and making memories instead of conjuring up the best way to document every social event for the post I'd rush to upload the next day.

This was the 2010s, the age of the thigh gap, and as a girl who just wasn't built like that, attaining one became an unhealthy obsession. But this didn't come out of nowhere; it had online origins. Pro-ana (pro-anorexia) content on Tumblr quickly became something I consumed daily in secret, compounding my self-consciousness. This type of content didn't just show skinny bodies, it romanticised and glorified eating disorders, and promoted a sense of competition between young girls. I didn't come across this type of harmful content intentionally, but when one of my closest friends started re-blogging this content on her own account, I involuntarily became a consumer too and began internalising the belief that my body should look like that. That my hip and rib bones should be prominent through my clothes, my thighs should feel the breeze between them in summer instead of rubbing together, my stomach should be concave without having to suck in. That I should monitor, track and assess everything I ate, and refuse to eat anything that these pages didn't allow. Discovering pro-ana content on Tumblr was the start of an eight-year journey of obsession, self-criticism, shame and fixation on my body and all its 'flaws' – an obsession that was born online. So many women and girls have fallen into the same mental trap, and with the rise of the algorithm it's getting harder to avoid the most damaging content.

When I meet Jane, her daughter Megan* has been in hospital for 537 days. She tells me frankly that Megan recently had her first drink of water in over a year and a half, and I try to conceal my shock. Until I met Jane, I didn't know the fear of consuming food can also extend to water in severe cases. I didn't know it was possible for someone to survive without drinking water for this amount of time. And in normal circumstances, it isn't. But in hospital, sixteen-year-old Megan is fed through a nasogastric tube, a feeding tube inserted through the nose that sends food down to the stomach. Even through a computer screen speaking to Jane on Zoom, I can sense her exhaustion, a mum desperately trying to help her

* Jane and Megan are not their real names.

daughter get better. But I can also see the fear in her eyes, the fear that this is completely beyond her or her daughter's control.

Megan's mum first knew something was wrong when Megan plucked her mole off her face because 'she wanted to have a symmetrical face' when she was just fourteen. When Jane recalls this to me, I can't help but notice this happened around the time that the inverted filter on TikTok was going viral. This filter would run a line down the centre of your face and show what your face looked like if it was mirrored. It led to teenage girls across the globe making videos purely for the purpose of seeing how symmetrical their faces were, with many of them capturing their own horror at the realisation of not having a face that is geometrically symmetrical – a facial feature that has been touted as a defining trait of supermodels.

Within months of this incident, Megan's parents discovered that she was making herself sick after eating. 'She had this thing about having a flat stomach and she was following people [online] doing exercise for a flat stomach.' Hearing this hit me hard, and I suddenly felt a sense of shame for all the times I've followed these tutorials myself. My own experiences of disordered eating grew out of my fixation on my stomach and thighs as 'problem areas', at the very same age as Megan. Now, just over ten years on from my first experiences of disordered eating, I had hoped that the next generation would have it better, and that the open conversations that social media encourages around mental health and body image would have led to a societal shift. But what I was hearing was the same story. For so many girls, the digital world still exists as a relentless cycle of self-degradation and comparison that they get helplessly stuck in, and for girls like Megan, this is having life-threatening consequences.

Jane believes that her daughter's use of social media is responsible for her developing anorexia, a condition which has the highest mortality rate of all psychiatric disorders. 'She thought she had certain syndromes, as when she felt something she would type it into Google. She typed in anorexia and then all the algorithms kept sending her more and more stuff about anorexia. I think that fear is generated in young minds from the things they're shown on social media.' Her suspicions aren't just saddening, they're correct. Social media platforms and their algorithmic design is actively fuelling a body image crisis in young people. In 2021, Meta whistle-blower Frances Haugen leaked evidence revealing that Instagram was actively promoting eating disorder content to young users and fuelling a rise of eating disorders in the process.[2] So not only do social media platforms fail to keep young users safe from this type of content, they also actively send it their way. A study by the Center for Countering Digital Hate found that when researchers set up new TikTok accounts with the age set to thirteen years old, and briefly paused on videos about mental health, within eight minutes the app showed content related to eating disorders.[3] Far from being something we consciously seek out, young girls are being shown what these algorithms suspect they will be interested in. The same way that addictive algorithms expose vulnerable people to content that promotes self-harm and suicide, the same technical mechanisms are at play when it comes to pushing users towards content that promotes eating disorders.

Growing up scrolling on hyper-personalised feeds that show us content based on who we are and what we might be more likely to engage with has a conditioning effect. If we see photos of underweight women every day, we will inevitably start to think that is the norm. If we see photos and videos of influencers who are using steroids to achieve impossible levels of muscle mass, that might become our new goal in the gym. If our favourite content creators constantly share edited posts, with skin free from pores, blemishes and creases, we're not to blame if we expect their skin to look like that in real life. The fact that body dysmorphic disorder is now commonly referred to as Snapchat dysmorphia shows just how deeply intertwined the relationship is between what we see online and our perception of our bodies.

It's becoming increasingly apparent that the constant viewing and consumption of unrealistic digital content is not just harmful but has rapidly become a public health issue. In 2022, the NHS hit a record, but not one worth celebrating – it was treating record numbers of young people for eating disorders.[4] It isn't only women and girls who experience negative impacts on their body image as a result of social media. More and more young men are becoming fixated on growing muscle mass and monitoring and sharing their 'progress' online. A study found that greater social media use among adolescents and young adults has been associated with symptoms of muscle dysmorphia.[5] You only have to speak to young men who go to the gym to realise quickly that relentless dissatisfaction and negative self-comparison is rife, and is a huge source of unhappiness in young men. Not only this, but unaccountable and insidious social media algorithms are instrumental in fuelling this obsession, and are fuelling a shadowy black market of muscle-enhancing drugs. The Center for Countering Digital Hate found that steroid-like drugs (SLDs) are promoted on TikTok, with male influencers who promote these potentially illegal drugs amassing 1.8 million followers.[6] Captions such as 'just tell your parents they're vitamins' or 'risk it' reveal the gaps for harm that dangerous content around body image is posing to our young people, and the health risks that they are taking in desperation to feel better about themselves.

The driving forces behind social media are comparison, performance and engagement. Image-based platforms like Instagram are designed to fuel comparison through their features, be it likes, comments or follows. This breeds a culture of intense scrutiny when it comes to bodies and our appearances. The very functionalities of visual-led platforms that have birthed the influencer – likes, comments, saves, follows – might seem natural but are designed with our psychological vulnerabilities in mind. These features trigger validation-seeking behaviour that we might not do if our social media platforms were designed to be more like community hubs, personal journals or educational spaces.

The Facebook 'like' button was introduced in 2009, and this was the beginning of our digital popularity contest, which we have all unwillingly entered. The element of feedback from peers is the feature which results in the most problematic outcomes for our self-esteem.[7] But why is our appearance so inextricable from our online popularity and why are body parts so vulnerable to becoming fashion trends online? Today, bodies aren't our homes, they're hot commodities to be marketed, sold and consumed online, leaving our self-esteem at the fingertips of scrolling strangers. Those who work at these platforms know this; Meta whistle-blower Frances Haugen admitted, 'Instagram is about social comparison and about bodies.' [8]

In the journal article 'Uploading your best self: Selfie editing and body dissatisfaction',[9] the authors write that objectification explains how media representations socialise women to internalise an observer's view on ourselves, and self-objectify ourselves, resulting in a negative body image. In doing so, we internalise objectifying messages about our bodies which place a greater emphasis on their appearance rather than how they feel or what they can do.

This is something I've known from adolescence. I remember the days of rushing home to log on to Facebook where we would post 'like for a rate' or 'comment for a rate'. The result of these obscure challenges was a grand revelation: whether or not our school crushes thought we were pretty. There are the 'thirst trap' selfies, photos where you deem yourself the most desirable to those you want to attract to 'trap' them, intended to suss out whether lust is reciprocated or not. Most of us won't go to the gym without documenting it online in some way. When I was sixteen, I decided to go on a no carb diet. After a three-hour rowing training session after school, I insisted to my mum that I only wanted a bowl of grapes for dinner. But on social media, this restrictive and unhealthy regime was something I took pride in, and gained attention and affirmation.

At one time, my bio on Twitter was 'I haven't had a pie in five months', a statement that didn't make much sense if you didn't know me personally, but affirmed to myself that people were watching, waiting for me to slip up and now that I had publicly committed, I couldn't give up. To do so would make me a failure. In the meantime, I would post daily selfies on Instagram in tight bodycons or leggings and sports bras as a way of tracking myself, surveilling myself whilst revelling in the comments I received as a result. My craving for external validation was insatiable, and I was stuck in this cycle for most of my adolescence. At the same time, I would post 'body goals' photos of anonymous women I found on Tumblr, writing captions that expressed my awe for their bodies and harsh discontent for my own.

This is a familiar experience for many millennial and Gen Z women who grew up online. Ellen Atlanta, author of *Pixel Flesh*, explains that 'To exist as a young woman today is to flounder in this sea of paradoxes. [. . .] It's to resent the images that envelop you on social media whilst obsessively consuming and recreating the same content.' For Kelsey, a 26-year-old from Hampshire, social media was a constant source of negative comparison that led to her developing an eating disorder, but praise from other people online would fuel a toxic cycle of restriction. 'When I'd post pictures on Instagram people would comment things like "omg your waist is so small". I'd feel such a sense of achievement, like I was one of those girls that could be envied,' she says. 'But when I look back on those pictures now I feel sad for the girl who tried to never let herself eat.' If you've never experienced disordered eating, you might not understand how posting selfies can fuel unhealthy habits. Aren't selfies an indication you're happy and confident in your appearance? Unfortunately not. Research has found that the more time you spend on Instagram, the more likely you are to suffer eating disorders such as orthorexia, which is an obsession with healthy eating, and can manifest as cutting out entire food groups, being obsessed with calorie counting or checking the ingredients of foods.[10] Not only that, but evidence also revealed that 17 per cent of teenage girls said the app made their eating disorders worse.[11]

External validation online shaped how I viewed and valued my body from a very young age. With each Instagram selfie post I felt seen and liked, but I couldn't give myself the same validation. As Mary McGill writes in *The Visibility Trap*, 'Selfies have a natural resonance for those for whom seeing themselves as they wish to be seen is still a struggle.'[12] It's no wonder that our teenage years are when most young women begin to take selfies and seek comfort in this form of self-presentation. While cynics might be quick to reduce this to plain vanity, I understand that selfies can also be a valuable form of self-expression and documentation of our growth into womanhood. At a time when we are torn between people's perceptions of us, feelings of who we ought to be and what society and our families and friends expect from us, our social media profiles can become a space where we define ourselves. My online visibility to my peers was different to the experience I felt in person with them. I felt more likeable, more desirable, more creative and unique through the reactions I would receive online, at an age when feeling these things is of vital importance for a sense of self. Feeling seen is why so many of us depend on social media to create communities where we feel accepted and respected, but in a visual digital economy where the main focus is our appearance, our infatuation with the reflection in the black mirror can be damaging in equal measure.

For we aren't just seeing ourselves, we are seeing others too, and the online sphere pits us against each other, with follower counts, likes and comments being constant digital reminders of how we are ranked in comparison. We are now experiencing humanity through images more than ever before. There is a running joke amongst women online that we have albums of before photos in our camera roll, but no after photos, with the anticipated post-gym transformation never coming. The fact that our digital footprints and personal camera rolls have become places where we surveil, judge and assess our bodies makes me feel uncertain about how liberatory the ability to hoard images of ourselves really is.

As David Lyon elaborates in *The Culture of Surveillance*, digital technologies have entrenched watching and being watched into our daily lives. Our smartphones have become a constant source of hyperawareness and self-scrutiny, which fuels continual assessments of our physical appearances. For a moment, pause and think about how many times today you've looked at yourself through a digital screen, be that on a work Zoom meeting, in a selfie, photos of yourself online or a video call with a loved one.

Admittedly, I find it near impossible to focus on the other person's face whenever I'm on FaceTime, no matter how much I love them. Looking at ourselves has become such a core part of our lives that it feels strange to not see your reflection for a day. This new reality breeds self-obsession, and it can make everyday life stressful and anxiety-inducing, to a degree that is not normal. Lola Christina Alao puts it best: 'We were never supposed to see our own faces this much.'[13] During the pandemic this reached an all-time high, where there was an immense rise in 'Zoom dysmorphia' due to the frequency at which we were perceiving ourselves and seeing our reflections. It is hardly surprising that in a digital culture centred on constantly viewing ourselves and others, where we see a record number of faces every day in that little black mirror of ours, that satisfaction with our appearances is dwindling and the ease with which we can identify new opportunities for self-maximisation is at an all-time high.

Being constantly seen, be that through our own selfies or other people's phones, has created a new level of interpersonal surveillance, both within our own minds and towards others. The awareness of being potentially watched at any moment, captured from a 'bad angle' or laughing candidly has instilled a fear in us to be seen with bodies that move and have bodily functions. For confining our bodies to the four walls of a screen in a still and often posed image is to obscure and erase the natural forms and fluxes of bodies. From cellulite, to breakouts, to stubble and wrinkles, we are pressured to conform to the unspoken rules of Instagram culture, where censorship of the natural body has become all too common. The ability to constantly see ourselves and others has brought with it a dangerous societal pressure to constantly look appealing, materialising in the form of paying excessive attention to our appearance and holding more value to this than anything else that makes us who we are. Similarly, those who fail to meet the standards of images of themselves they present online are publicly shamed. Being called a 'catfish' was probably one of the worst things I could have imagined happening to me at the age of seventeen and I'm embarrassed to say would still hurt my feelings today. The paradoxical cycle is coming around again now too. The same women who have put fillers in their face to look better in images are being criticised for looking fake or having 'pillow face' (a swollen face) in real life. Beauty in today's digital age is a game no woman can win.

But there are those who are winning a completely different game, because they designed it, wrote the rules and gave themselves the upper hand. The first version of Facebook, called FaceMash, was created by Mark Zuckerberg while at Harvard University so he and his friends could rate the 'hotness' of the women at their universities. By taking their online photos without consent and putting them side by side with another woman, the platform was the original 'hot or not'. Whilst writing the software, a blog entry he posted read: 'I almost want to put some of these faces next to pictures of farm animals and have people vote on which is more attractive.'[14]

The objectification of women's bodies runs deep within Silicon Valley. A *Guardian* investigation found that Microsoft and Google's artificial intelligence algorithms associate women's bodies with being sexually provocative. An analysis of hundreds of photos of men and women in underwear, exercising and even pregnant, found that women were tagged by the algorithm as sexual. A comparison of the 'racy score' given to an image of two men and two women in underwear found a huge discrepancy – the image of the men was just 14 per cent whereas the image of the women was 96 per cent.[15]

Furthermore, an investigation in 2020 found that Instagram favours photos of men and women dressed showing more skin (*unless* your body does not conform to Eurocentric beauty standards).[16] Our digital culture mirrors the offline world's culture, and the objectifying misogyny that women are subject to in society is reinforced online by social media platforms due to their disproportionate focus on our appearances. Worse still, Big Tech cash in as they amplify biases, platform unattainable beauty standards and further reinforce disillusionment of self for many men, women and girls.

To illustrate exactly how the digital sphere has worsened the landscape for women, we can look at how women's bodies are subject to the unforgiving scrutiny of trend cycles. Now, this is nothing new and has been the case throughout history; however, today we see these trends happening at a pace that is impossible to keep up with. These 'body parts as fashion' trends are what author Emma Dabiri calls 'beauty standards on speed'.[17] The immense volume of content being generated and shared into our digital ether means trends come and go quickly, so what might be fashionable today could be trash tomorrow. The same way that fast fashion companies and their overproduction meant that we went from having four seasons to fifty-two seasons, fashion and beauty trends now come and go within days. The internal pressure of having to keep up is exhausting because even if you don't consciously follow these trends, we are seeing them, breathing them, living them. We don't speak enough about how taxing it is to be constantly told what products to consume and which procedures to undergo by individuals who don't have to pay for them and are even paid to promote them. If it isn't our pores, it's our stomach, if it isn't our stomach it's our hairline, if it isn't our hairline it's our lips, and if it isn't our outer appearance it's our gut health, our pH levels, our blood sugar. There is always something to fix next.

There is a snowball effect to this, and it is no surprise that the rise of digital technology can be mapped on to the rise of surgical procedures that were previously limited to the realm of celebrities and A-listers, including BBLs (Brazilian butt lifts), breast enhancements and tweakments (including facial fillers and lifts). The people who have these procedures often then go on to profit from sharing them as 'natural' to the masses who then want to emulate them, thus continuing the cycle. Bella Hadid's transformation is a prime example of the faux natural beauty that social media idolises. On the surface, her look gives the impression of an effortless beauty, but the reality is a lot of money, surgical procedures and high-market treatments are needed to maintain her face, which arguably has come to be her most valuable asset as the face of million-dollar brands including Bvlgari, Dior and Charlotte Tilbury. Many filters we see on social media have been carved out to mirror her feline features, lifting our brow and cheekbones and slimming our jawline. One UK doctor revealed that Hadid's face was the 'most requested' by clients in 2021, with many of these requests coming from teenagers.[18]

It's now the norm for us to be bombarded with the latest 'aesthetic' relentlessly online, a look we ought to aspire to, a lifestyle to emulate. In the summer of 2023, I took myself to Waterstones for a writing day. It was busy, being the school holidays, with parents trying their hardest to entertain their teens and manage their toddlers. Being the people watcher I am, I couldn't help but observe a mum and daughter who sat on the table beside me in the café. While her mum asked what her daughter wanted to do that day, the daughter was on her phone. When she opened TikTok to scroll, I noticed the first video that was on her feed was titled 'How to be *that* girl'. As she swiped on the carousel of images, I was sad to see each one being a suggestion of a beauty or skincare product, all adding to a likely overflowing list of how she could be better. As if spending her pocket money on skincare would allow her to be one step closer to her best self (or the best self the algorithm had destined for her). No longer are we allowed to just exist, we must always be on the pursuit of self-improvement. As articulated by writer Jess White, 'The incessant and insane categorisation of every single little feeling a human can have as entire personality model is entirely down to content-ifying our lives and the "branding" that individuals build themselves. It all boils down to consumption.'[19]

Social media shows us a very limited category of bodies, but it also reinforces age-old biases and hierarchies of which bodies are socially acceptable, and which can never be beautiful. In 2019, there was backlash when queer people and people of colour realised Instagram was shadow-banning their content on the platform.[20] Fat bodies are also subject to policing on the app, with plus-sized content creators like Nyome Nicholas-Williams highlighting the double standards of what body types Instagram deems acceptable and what goes against Instagram guidelines. When a photo of Nyome topless with her arms covering her breasts was taken down by the platform, her followers mobilised to start a petition calling out the platform's shadowban, which gained over 20,000 signatures.[21]

The same Westernised and fatphobic beauty stand-ards, which have been ingrained throughout history in the offline world, transcend our digital boundaries and are reinforced by algorithms that replicate those same prejudices. At the same time, whilst social media cham-pions would argue that wider representation of diverse body types and shapes online has positively influenced our relationships to our bodies, the reality is that simply seeing more bodies doesn't make us any happier with our own. In fact, the 'representational revolution' has failed to bring us liberation from body image issues, due to the systemic pressures and overemphasis on our physical traits that all women face.

Our bodies have always been more than physical vessels. Throughout history we have embellished them, trained them, painted them, and these are all attempts to communicate who we are to the wider world. But on social media, it's less about what we want to do and more about what everyone else is doing. Many of us – willingly or unwillingly – subscribe to relentless pressure to fit into the hottest new aesthetic, even if only to perform this online. The longer we spend online, wishing to look like others, the more adverts are sold to us via these apps. We must understand that Big Tech companies profit from all of this pressure.

It is young people who are facing a widespread crisis of self because of their immersion in the digital sphere. Social media plays an essential role in young people's social and personal lives and so it shapes their sense of self in profound ways. From the things they believe, to the hobbies they adopt, to the way they view themselves, the impact on young minds and behaviour cannot be under-played. Today, before most children have gone through puberty, they are in possession of a highly complex yet easy to use means of technology: a fifth of three- to four-year-olds have a smartphone.[22] While children are going through profound physical and mental changes in the transition into adolescence, they are being immersed into a visual economy that encourages and even promotes harmful behaviours. Online, young people are being bombarded with an endless stream of images of people whose appearances require teams of stylists, dieticians and make-up artists, an unattainable level of wealth to expend on beauty regimens and physical upkeep, and the disposable time required to maintain their appearance. It's no wonder that teenage girls then feel inadequate and not enough. For example, 51 per cent of girls aged from seven to ten are very happy with how they look, but this drops to 16 per cent by the time they are between eleven and sixteen.[23]

So much of the digital content teenage girls and boys see today pressures them to focus totally on their appearance and what is on the surface. Be it young boys seeing figures like Andrew Tate and Logan Paul who promote a macho one-size-fits-all idea of masculine beauty, or teen girls who see young women altering their faces before they've even grown into their own, the digital sphere's impact is unrelenting and it isn't going anywhere. I grew up as part of the first generation who had access to apps like Instagram and Facebook as a teenager, and I can say that the impact on my body image and confidence was detrimental to say the least. But now, things are even more advanced. Primary school children are asking for skincare for Christmas, teenagers are getting Botox and filler.

In a report that charity Global Action Plan released on children's use of social media, they looked at how the use of social media can encourage children to focus on extrinsic goals rather than intrinsic goals.[24] Extrinsic goals include things we see online all the time – making money, being attractive, having social recognition in the form of followers and fans. Our intrinsic goals include things that are internal to our wellbeing, like self-acceptance, affiliation and community. Sadly, extrinsic goals are what has come to define good content. It's much easier to create an engaging TikTok that has the potential to go viral when you own nice things and live in an aesthetically pleasing space, or quite frankly, if you are beautiful.

In a visual economy where our images are viewed as a measure of our worth, it's no wonder that young people feel increasing pressure to look a certain way. Social media is encouraging children to want to become adults far too early, and is harming their perceptions of themselves in the process. A 2023 poll by Girlguiding UK found that the happiness of girls and young women is at the lowest level since 2009, with body image and the effects of social media being one of the main concerns mentioned by young girls.[25] Social media has exposed us to more bodies and faces than we could ever be expected to process. How then can they expect to protect themselves from the unconscious comparison that comes with overexposure?

Protective legislation is failing to keep up with the scale of the problem as well as the impacts it's having on our physical and mental health. Dr Chukwuemeka Nwuba, who is a London-based mental health doctor and editor of *Eating Disorders Don't Discriminate* told me of one of his 24-year-old female patients, who, when he asked them if they used any pro-ana websites, they responded, 'Yeah, Twitter.' 'This massively took me by surprise and made me realise that we shouldn't be focused on the underground illicit pro-ana sites. These are the least of our worries. Some of the world's biggest social media companies – which have negligible safeguards in my opinion – are where many are getting their destructive content from.' He has also had inpatients voluntarily hand in their phones to staff, acknowledging that time spent online would undermine their therapy and treatment. This is nothing short of a public health crisis, and one whose digital roots have gone ignored for far too long.

Harmful content exists on a spectrum and can take on many forms. An overedited selfie from a famous influencer may be just as harmful as content that promotes diet culture. Social media algorithms don't differentiate, and are intent upon feeding you more content, no matter the cost. One thing that Jane told me about her daughter's use of social media, which sums up a lot of parents' worries about the online world, is that 'she believed everything on the internet to be true'. The unregulated nature of social media has meant that we are constantly bombarded with unrealistic standards of beauty that are often total misrepresentations in themselves. There is no label to say whether a photo is edited, or back story to describe the painful surgery that allowed someone to look a certain way. And so, young people are continually at risk of falling victim to inaccurate depictions of bodies believing them to be true or a fair reflection of the average person.

There have been some changes. In 2021, influencers were told by the Advertising Standards Agency that they can no longer use misleading filters on beauty adverts.[26] However, this doesn't go far enough, and we need to address the problem at the root. Social media platforms should implement a feature that shows whether editing apps were used before uploading the image. This would be a step towards regaining our grasp over reality and accepting our bodies for what they are in their natural form. Another way that we can collectively combat the idea that bodies are no more than decorative objects to be perfected and curated is through creating and sharing digital content that demonstrates otherwise. Dr Chukwuemeka Nwuba believes that banning harmful hashtags that promote eating disorders, and instead subsidising content creators who share positive and educational information around body image, is one easy way social media platforms could counter the harmful impacts that social media has had on young people's body image.

The fact that I spent a huge amount of time in my adolescence seeking out validation from others online on the basis of my physical appearance, in the form of likes and comments, has trickled into my sense of self-worth as an adult. I still struggle to decipher between posting for approval and that instant gratification that comes with notifications and posting things to genuinely connect and share. This is something we need to acknowledge so that we can heal from it. Being able to distinguish between these motivations to post empowers us to be intentional with our use of social media. In this way, we can share content and insights into our life that help others and that are vulnerable and honest, instead of feeding into cycles of comparison and self-criticism.

Logging off is another way we can heal. I often find comfort in going offline, taking in the range of bodies and faces around me. Going on holiday as a teen, beaches were a place of fear for many years as I would worry how my body would look and be perceived by others in swimwear. I would have intrusive thoughts of what my body looked like from behind and I felt terrified that I looked revolting and that everyone was thinking it too. As an adult, I still feel nervous when I think about the phrase 'beach body' because those immense and unattainable pressures, as well as the self-hatred that consumed me as a teenager, come flooding back. But now, when I am on the beach, or on holiday, I recognise how significantly reality differs from my perception, a perception built by social media. 'When you're around so many different body types, bodies start to mean less and less,' Annie Lord writes.[27] Simply take a walk down any high street and you'll realise that the offline world is not nearly as curated and 'perfect' as our timelines.

In 2019, I had a photo taken of me on holiday. I had felt confident at the time, and happy in myself. But, only a year or so later, when I had developed a range of interests beyond my unhealthy obsession with the gym, I archived (hid) the post. Part of me felt embarrassed to keep it up on my profile, as if my now less-toned body made me a liar or a cheat. As if I didn't deserve to relish the joy I had felt in that time of my life any more. I unarchived that photo while writing this chapter. Bodies are fluid, but the highly intricate curation of our digital archives suggest otherwise. Stills of images captured at calculated angles give us a false sense of what bodies look like when the reality is that they're moving, breathing, relaxing, living. They are flawed, complex, bumpy, muscly, hairy and always changing. My body might not look the same in every photo I've ever taken, but it's still the same body, and it's my home.

CHAPTER 8

Misogyny's Newer Model

'I fucking hate feminists and they should all die and burn in hell.'

Microsoft's AI-powered Twitter account Tay after
sixteen hours online[1]

'I know you're not where you said you were.'

That was the message that made Katie* realise something was wrong. Her relationship with her ex had ended around a year previously, and whilst they stayed in contact to co-parent their son, she kept him at a distance. To say they had ended on bad terms would be putting it lightly. Her ex was controlling and coercive, and since the break-up there had been multiple instances of him trying to get back at her for ending the relationship. An email smear campaign claiming she was a bad mother to their only son sent out to friends, family and colleagues was

---

* Katie is not her real name.

just one example of what she had already been subject to at the whim of his unstable and manipulative behaviour. At first, she tried to brush the message off, telling herself that he was bluffing. This wasn't the first time he had tried to play mind games with her. But the bluntness of his message pushed her to bring it up to a friend at the time. 'He's either tracking your phone or tracking your car,' her friend told her plainly, already knowing what he was capable of. Katie laughed it off, but this comment planted a seed of doubt. She decided to take precautions.

After searching her car for a physical device and finding nothing, she was left baffled. But the next time she absent-mindedly picked up her phone, she saw the Land Rover InControl App. This app allows customers to access breakdown services, information about mileage and registration, as well as a car's GPS location. Katie suddenly realised that her abuser wasn't using a physical device to track her, but a digital one. It was an app that had been designed to keep her car safe, and now was making her entirely unsafe. To test her theory, Katie switched phones and downloaded the app again, which allowed her to get into her car's account without any challenges or security hurdles, meaning her abuser could have done the exact same. After weeks of pleading back and forth with the manufacturer, Katie was finally able to have the GPS tracker switched off. But what she thought might offer a respite from his abuse backfired. Their childcare arrangements for co-parenting included her ex agreeing to keep his location turned on for her to see on WhatsApp on days where he would look after their son. 'The day after we managed to switch off the GPS on the Range Rover app, he turned off his [WhatsApp] location. I know it's because I took away his ability to track me.' Katie had acted to keep her and her son safe, and she was being punished by her abuser.

This may just sound like one calculating abusive ex, but this specific type of digital violence has a name – technology-facilitated abuse – and it's on the rise. From spying on exes, to sending abusive messages and email smear campaigns, to leaking intimate images, or photographing without consent, the failure to safeguard digital technologies and apply protections the same way we do offline has led to opportunistic abusers taking advantage. This abuse is so prolific that it's creating a crisis in domestic abuse support services, with their capacity being stretched as it is due to budget cuts to women's services. In 2017, domestic violence charity Refuge had to form a specialist tech-facilitated abuse team due to the rising need for support relating to this type of abuse, and between 2018 and 2022, they saw an increase of 258 per cent of survivors being supported by the team.[2] 'It's really unlikely now to work with a case of stalking or harassment where tech *isn't* the facilitator,' says Emma Pickering, who leads the team.

In the digital age, women are losing on multiple fronts. The beauty standards and body shaming on digital platforms are compromising young minds and negatively impacting mental health, and these same platforms are radically reducing our safety from those who seek to harm us. Blind spots in legislation and oversights in design have increased the risk of violence and abuse. Technology has only emboldened abusers to take their violence and hatred to new levels, with erasable digital footprints granting them a different type of impunity in the process. This form of online harm isn't just a matter of bad users, it is bias and lack of forethought in the design.

It isn't just smartphones that have enabled this rise in digital abuse. Abusers are also using smart devices to harass their victims. Many of us now own a smart device, the friendly little gadgets that sit in room corners like personal assistants waiting at our beck and call. You might tell your Alexa to turn off the lights from the comfort of your bed at night, or check that the delivery you've been anticipating for weeks has finally been dropped off through your Ring camera. When national treasure Alison Hammond pulled her phone out live during *This Morning* to answer her Ring doorbell for her postman, it was a hilarious yet noteworthy moment where I came to the realisation of the central role that these all-seeing tools have come to have in our lives. Despite the added convenience these tools bring, the smart home is increasingly becoming a privacy risk for all of us, and for domestic abuse victims, a physical safety risk. When two professors of internet technology (who are also both hackers) were asked by the German Ministry of Law and Consumer Protection what they thought was the greatest danger in the commercial world, their answer was unanimous: smart homes.[3] For victims of domestic abuse, smart homes are easy entry points for abusers, though they are sold to us with the promise to make our spaces safer.

As a victim of abuse, Katie believed she was making a wise decision when she installed a smart device in her home to further document potential abuse to provide to the police as evidence of his abuse. Her ex would regularly turn up at her doorstep unannounced, so she wanted to be prepared for the worst. She bought a Hive camera, which detects movement, sound and even specific people. But soon after installing it, Katie was horrified to realise that her ex was tormenting her again, this time as if he were within the walls of her home. 'All of a sudden, he messaged me quoting a couple of things that I knew that I hadn't told anyone, except one friend when she was at mine for dinner. I hadn't said it outside of the house and I wasn't on the phone.'

Her ex had hacked into her Hive camera, and with this access her abuser was not only able to track her physical movements, but listen to her conversations with friends, family and colleagues inside her home too. As soon as she realised he had hacked into this digital device, she unplugged it, but this resulted in another form of power play. 'Whenever I would find the source of a leak and get rid of it, he would retaliate in some way.' This time, the retaliations included hacking her Facebook and email accounts, deleting important emails from her inbox and making random restaurant bookings which would flood her inbox. It made her daily life a living hell, one that no one understood the gravity of, because the only one who could see all of the abuse was her. With digital technology, the physical trails of abuse are often invisible, or easily erased by the abuser. Abusers are not just enabled by their technology, they are actively empowered by it. Their exploitation of tech means digital devices become an armoury at their disposal.

For five years, Katie has been stuck in a cycle of abuse and control. Despite reporting her ex to the police multiple times, she has been met with pushback, being told repeatedly that there isn't enough evidence. This is despite the fact that she has a log with almost 200 entries, spanning from 2018 to 2023 of each incident, stored away for the day she might be able to afford taking legal action against him. You would think that this would be more than enough to prove a pattern of abuse and harm to the police. But currently, prosecution rates for technology-facilitated abuse are dismally low. In the UK to date, there has only been one conviction so far for this type of abuse. What does this tell women who are experiencing abuse that isn't leaving bruises on their bodies and abrasions on their skin? What reassurance does this offer when those who are meant to keep us safe are not equipped to cope with the growing evolution of abuse in today's digital world? The power gap between victims and perpetrators continues to widen in the digital age, while legislative and legal safeguards that could protect us are painfully slow to catch up. Katie tells me that fighting this process and trying to seek help has felt like a losing battle, simply because services do not have the knowledge or funding to tackle this type of domestic abuse. 'The courts, the police, CAFCASS, they don't understand how abusers are using the technology, they don't understand the behaviour or why they're doing it.' We are struggling to uphold safety in our digital spheres, and the problem is not going anywhere.

When explicit deepfake images of Taylor Swift went viral on X in 2024, being viewed 47 million times before their removal, it was an alarming reminder that no woman is safe online. Image-based sexual abuse is a fast-growing crime whereby abusers use technology to share intimate content without consent. From pornographic deepfakes to so-called 'revenge porn', image-based sexual abuse is rife. In the UK between 2018 and 2021, almost 19,000 cases of image-based sexual abuse were reported to the police, and 80 per cent of these victims were women and girls.[4] Non-consensual sharing doesn't just happen on porn platforms like you might think. A report in 2019 found that each month, Meta receives around 500,000 user removal requests of sensitive and sexual images on their platforms.[5] 'It's a whole ecosystem of abuse,' Elena Michael, director of Not Your Porn tells me. 'You've got the creators of this content; you've got the people that initially take the content and share it; but then you've got the people that share it on; then you've got the closed groups. Some survivors we've spoken to have had whole fan groups for their non-consensual content.' Far from a niche issue, image-based sexual abuse is part of the wider culture of objectification that manifests and is encouraged online.

Ellesha knows this better than most. In 2018, she and her boyfriend broke up; their relationship had not been an easy one and he had cheated on her multiple times. However, when Ellesha found out he had been sending nude photographs to a friend of hers, it was the final straw. The relief she felt with the end of the relationship, when it finally did end, was only temporary. Five months after their relationship broke down while on holiday with her parents, Ellesha was contacted by his latest ex-girlfriend to make her aware that she had found an account under his name on Pornhub. What followed next not only ruined a family holiday but scarred Ellesha for life. His profile was filled with videos of Ellesha and her ex having sex, which had now accumulated thousands of views from strangers across the world. Not only this, but Ellesha didn't even know these videos existed. Her ex had been filming her during sex without her consent or knowledge. With degrading titles like 'fucking the ex', Ellesha was horrified that videos of her in a deeply intimate moment, one she thought was private, were now available for the whole world to see. 'It was a huge shock. I didn't even realise that they existed, let alone that they'd been on the internet for months without me knowing,' Ellesha tells me.

As soon as she had landed back in the UK, Ellesha went to her local police station to report the crime. After having to retell her account of this traumatic experience, she was told that the police are not able to access Pornhub from their servers, and in order to have evidence, she would need to collect it herself. Imagine the trauma of experiencing this type of abuse, and then being told that you would need to go through the painstakingly time-consuming and emotionally intensive process of screen recording your own evidence. After a long month of waiting and chasing the police for updates, he was finally arrested. The police even let Ellesha know that her ex was being pursued by another police force in the UK for doing the same thing to another woman, and this gave her the hope that prosecution would be fairly straightforward given this wasn't a one-off, but she was very quickly disappointed.

'The CPS said there wasn't enough to charge him,' Ellesha tells me. You would have thought that multiple videos and more than one victim reporting this abuse by her ex would have been sufficient evidence, but you'd be wrong. Despite the surge in image-based sexual abuse and criminality being enshrined in law, only 3 per cent of incidents have resulted in a charge.[6] The failure to prosecute cases of digital violence and abuse is breeding a silent epidemic of online harm, leaving victims to fend for themselves without support or justice.

Ellesha felt totally alone in her fight, until one morning when she heard Kate Isaacs, founder of campaigning organisation Not Your Porn speaking on Radio 1. In 2019, one of Kate's friends had her iCloud account hacked and her images were uploaded on to Pornhub, being down-loaded thousands of times in the process. The failure of Pornhub to respond and remove the videos and images led her to start a campaign against non-consensual sharing and image-based sexual abuse, which resulted in her forcing Pornhub to remove millions of non-consensual videos from the platform.[7] Ellesha immediately reached out to Kate, and not long after was interviewed about her experiences on the radio. To her surprise, despite previously having been assured there was not enough evidence to prosecute, her appearance in the media (and undoubtedly the warranted criticism it galvanised towards the police force) led to them reopening the case. This time the case was under their cybercrime team, with more resources and staff dedicated to her case, a decision that should have been made from the day she reported the crime. 'They did a big delve into his online activity so they could show without a shadow of a doubt that this email address that he used to upload the video on to Pornhub he used for everything else.' Unsurprisingly, everything went back to his IP address. 'We went over my statements in more detail. We worked hard. But they needed to find something completely new to rearrest to confiscate his devices.' After another two months' wait, the CPS decided yet again not to charge, but the letter justifying the decision was more painful than the decision itself. 'The letter questioned if we [victims] were telling the truth and whether we were reliable witnesses. It questioned our morals. There were things in there like "Yes it's linked back to his IP address but he lives with his brother and his parents, so they could have uploaded it." It felt like they were making excuses for him.' Our collective understanding of digital abuse is lagging far behind and similarly to abuse cases offline, victim blaming remains prevalent.

It isn't only police who are ill-equipped to deal with new forms of abuse in the digital age, but the very platforms that profit from these online harms have been slow to act to end them. When Matthew's ex-partner impersonated him on the dating platform Grindr after they broke up, over 1,400 people were sent to his home address and place of work over ten months. When someone leaks your personal information such as address and phone number it is called doxxing, and in this case, the doxxing led to physical attacks, stalking and people even trying to break into his home. 'What is supposed to be an exciting, new age of technology leading the force behind the way humans connect and interact has had an adverse effect on my life. Through the weaponisation of technology, I was left completely disarmed and vulnerable.'

Despite complaining to Grindr, emailing, calling and even getting his friends and family to do the same, the app refused to act. When Matthew tried to hold Grindr to account for putting his physical safety at risk, they argued this was not their responsibility due to Section 230 of the Communications Decency Act, which means platforms are not classified as publishers of content, and that the responsibility of content safety instead lies with users. Is there any other industry that can so blatantly fail to meet the bare minimum of keeping customers safe, and then proceed to blame the customer? It's like buying medicine that is contaminated, taking it and falling ill and the pharmaceutical company saying that it's the consumer's fault for choosing to take the medication. Tech companies and platforms wrap themselves in blankets of impunity, shielded by wealth and political clout, but users pay the price. When it comes to sexual violence, something that continues to be ignored offline, the opportunities for harm continue to arise online whilst companies remain unaccountable.

Katie, Ellesha and Matthew's stories are just scratching the surface of this world and now we are beginning to see similar tales in the media. Image-based sexual abuse became a national campaign when *Love Island* star Georgia Harrison took her ex-partner Stephen Bear to court for the crime. Bear had uploaded an intimate video of them on his OnlyFans account, and soon after, 'Georgia Harrison sex tape' became a top Google search.[8] After waiving her right to anonymity, her campaigning led to a monumental change in the law. This change removed the need for there to be an intent to cause distress or humiliation in order for non-consensual sharing to be prosecuted, giving victims across the country a better chance of justice. Survivors like Ellesha and Georgia are fighting to make image-based sexual abuse a thing of the past. Since Ellesha's experience, she has joined Not Your Porn as a campaigner, an organisation that links survivors to support services, offers legal advice, trains victims to speak to the police and organises peer-to-peer support groups. Campaigning enables survivors to regain control where it has previously been taken from them. Channelling her disappointment in the system into campaigning with Not Your Porn has helped Ellesha to heal from the trauma of having her intimate images shared online, and allowed her to pass on her own understanding to other victims in need of support. 'I would have been completely lost and wouldn't be the person I am today if Kate had not helped me in the way she did.'

In her podcast, *High Low*, model Emily Ratajkowski describes the binary nature of how our devices can be used as either a weapon or a shield. For women, the notion that our digital devices are a double-edged sword is even more familiar, and we all have our stories. When I was sixteen, I was travelling on the bus to college when I noticed the man sitting opposite me holding his phone oddly vertical and pointing it towards me and all the other young girls on the bus on multiple occasions, tapping in the centre of the screen every few minutes. For the entire bus journey, I watched to make sure that I was certain of what I had suspected. When I reached my stop, I called him out. I shouted at him to show me the photos he had been taking and delete them, threatening to take a photo of him and expose him online. After denying and pleading, my threat to send his photo to the police was finally enough to scare him into admitting taking photos of multiple children without consent, and he finally deleted the images in front of me. It is a memory that has stayed with me forever, and I often get bouts of paranoia when I see men holding their phones at a certain angle in public towards women they don't know. Given that upskirting – the process by which someone uses equipment to take a photo up someone's skirt without consent – only became a crime in 2019 following the determined campaigning of activist Gina Martin, it's clear that women are at greater risk of having technology weaponised against them, for the very reason that gender-based violence is so endemic in our offline world.

In a desperate attempt to keep themselves safe, most women I know avoid posting stories until they've left a location, for the very reason that it enables abusers to target them. After I was sexually assaulted and harassed as a student at university, I knew all too well why. By watching my Snapchat stories and connecting the dots from what he knew about where I lived, he started to stalk me. He showed up at my gym using his friend's code when he knew I was there. He followed me home afterwards, pleading with me to invite him in, until I threatened to call the police and he finally left me alone. Not long after, on a summer's day, students filled the grassy banks outside the library, drinking ciders and iced coffee between lectures. Before heading to meet a friend to study together, I took a quick photo of the view and posted it on my Instagram story, not thinking twice. Within minutes, I had a message in my DMs. 'Are you at the library?' My heart dropped. He had watched my story and now had a good idea of where I was. I ignored the message and headed to meet my friend. But fear flooded through me when I saw him enter the library just minutes after me. I ducked my head under our table and urged her, 'We need to leave.' She reassured me that he hadn't seen us and we quickly gathered our laptops and packed to go, but as we were walking out and down the steps – another Instagram notification. It was a direct message from him, and he had sent me an expiring photo. Not sure what to expect, I clicked to open it. At first, I wasn't sure what I was looking at as it seemed to just be the library steps taken from the top. But then I noticed it was a photo of me live in that moment, rushing hurriedly down the library steps. On it, he had typed, 'I see you.'

On the other side of the same coin, women continue to resist, creatively using the tools being weaponised against them to confront their oppressors head-on. One example of this is the viral message template that has been used by women across the world to intimidate men who cyberflash them, which recently became a crime following the Online Safety Act. The message reads: 'AUTOREPLY: We have detected the transmission of unsolicited pornographic images of potentially illegal nature [code:36489-a] and your device's IP address has been forwarded to the police department pending an investigation. If you think this is a mistake, reply STOP.' Scrambling in panic mode, women share screenshots of their perpetrators spamming STOPPPP, taking joy in this act of collective resistance rather than letting men silence us. #MeToo is undeniably the most high-profile example of digital feminist activism, with the phrase first being used on MySpace in 2006 by survivor and grassroots activist Tarana Burke, and which later went viral following the sexual abuse allegations against Harvey Weinstein in 2017. Social media has undeniably offered us a new medium through which to connect with other women, overcome geographical barriers and build international movements through our shared experiences of womanhood and show that we will not be silenced.

Women with an understanding of the lived experiences of survivors are often the creators of the digital innovation that women want and need. Hera Hussain is someone who has done just that. Helping two friends get out of abusive relationships, she realised the sheer scale of challenges in accessing online support for victims of domestic abuse, particularly for women of colour. 'All the ways the charity sector was set up were so traditional and I couldn't find support for my friend in the way that I thought I should have been able to. Everything was helpline-based, their websites were just like PR sheets, there was nothing for survivors on there, and we were going online because my friend was scared to speak to someone on the phone or in an office.' Similarly, resources she did find online often excluded these women further. 'A lot of the resources I did find were very monocultural, they weren't very inclusive, and they sometimes had quite racist stereotypes around different communities.' This led her to create Chayn, which now provides free online trauma-informed resources that are survivor-written and approved by therapists in fourteen languages, which have been used by over 500,000 people across the globe. Alecto AI is a survivor-created app which allows people who have been the victims of image-based sexual abuse to remove their photos, something that platforms are consistently slow at doing. These female founders and the digital services they have created both reclaim agency into the hands of those who have been harmed in the digital world and empower them to fight back.

Technology-facilitated abuse and image-based sexual abuse are more visceral examples of what a culture of misogyny means for women and girls in our digital world. But the sexist trolling and abuse that we see daily on the internet exists in the same world. Online, misogyny is a spectacle. Its advocates are championed and amplified as being unapologetic free speakers who are simply stating what many others are thinking. Their content manifests as talk show lites, with these podcast bros ruling the manosphere with their unapologetic sexism and misogyny, becoming mini-celebrities in the process. The viral potential of degradation and humiliation of women online has been personified by Andrew Tate. Racking up more Google searches than the Queen, Kim Kardashian and Donald Trump combined in just a month, you'd expect someone with this much cultural capital to be equally inspiring and empowering, or so you'd hope. But no. Andrew Tate is a misogynistic influencer who rose to digital fame sharply in 2022 for his outrageous views on women, and was later charged with human trafficking, rape and forming an organised crime group linked to sexually exploiting women. Before these charges, many of the women who had heard how he spoke about us had suspected that his ill treatment of women extended beyond 'just words'. In one video describing how he would react if accused of cheating by a woman, he says, 'It's bang out the machete, boom in her face and grip her by the neck. Shut up, bitch.' Some of his other beliefs include that rape victims should 'bear responsibility for his attacks' and that women are a man's property.

While these statements sound like they come from the darkest corners of the internet, Tate is no niche and his views are no longer fringe, but are fast becoming popular beliefs. His videos have billions of views and have a significant impact on young boys and men. In 2024, polling found that Gen Z men are more likely than baby boomers to believe that feminism has done more harm than good.[9] Though progressive social movements have made strides in our physical world in recent years, the tide of antifeminism is building in the digital age.

My friend has an eight-year-old son, and he is already being exposed to misogynistic content on TikTok and YouTube, leaving her deeply worried about how these views are shaping his view of women and their place in the world. 'I had never heard of Andrew Tate and suddenly I got a call from a friend who said she heard my son talking about him. After googling and finding out who he was, I was slightly shocked and horrified. When I asked him about it, he said, "He is funny and he has lots of cars."' Figures like Tate are radicalising boys into sexist ideologies before they've hit puberty. Even teachers have flocked to the forum Reddit to voice their concerns on how Tate and others like him are shaping young boys' minds and attitudes to women, with one example of boys refusing to take tests from women teachers.[10]

Sexist and degrading narratives that figures like Andrew Tate peddle on social media are directly linked to the epidemic of online harassment against women and girls. When I interviewed Naomi Klein about her latest book *Doppelganger*, she said something utterly profound that opened my eyes to the root causes of online harassment and the toxicity of our digital ecosystem. Online, people don't just forget to 'be kind', but the design of social media actively incentivises us to do the opposite. 'There is a necessary partitioning that happens [online] where you're creating this publicly consumable self [. . .] you're creating a product version of yourself. [. . .] The problem with creating a thing version of you is that people will mistake it for a thing and they'll start to treat you as a thing. They'll throw hard objects at you and think you won't bleed.'

Online, people are not treated as they would be in the offline world, and they are not held to account for their words and actions in the way they would be offline. At the same time, algorithms built for increasing user engagement amplify abusive and violent content and give those individuals a platform for their hate. In the attention economy, abusers – I believe the word 'troll' fails to call them what they really are – are actively rewarded through likes and views, making them feel empowered and popular. It's no wonder that some atrocious cases of terrorism have been livestreamed for 'fans' to see, revealing the very problem with a digital culture that equates visibility with value and attention with praise.

According to Amnesty International, online abuse happens to a woman every thirty seconds on X alone.[11] Women who are seen to voice their opinions are more at risk of being targeted online, which explains why politicians, activists and journalists are at more risk of doxxing.[12] As Laurie Penny articulates so perfectly, for women, 'An opinion, it seems, is the short skirt of the internet. Having one and flaunting it is somehow asking an amorphous mass of almost entirely male keyboard-bashers to tell you how they'd like to rape, kill and urinate on you.'[13]

Online abuse is an intersectional issue where our vulnerability to it is dependent on factors of race, gender, sexuality and ability. The Center for Democracy and Technology found that women of colour candidates in the US 2020 general elections were most likely to be targeted with sexist abuse, racist abuse and violent abuse online.[14] It's been well documented that Diane Abbott, the UK's first Black female MP, receives almost a third of all abusive tweets directed at Britain's female MPs.[15] For those who experience discrimination offline, the online world can present new risks of abuse which have become unacceptable in our physical world, for the very reason that it grants individuals a toxic combination of anonymity and a lack of accountability. In 2024, a Sky News investigation found that Zarah Sultana, the youngest Muslim MP ever elected in the UK, receives the most online hate of all MPs, with her saying that abuse increased after she expressed her solidarity with the Palestinian cause.[16] Despite its prevalence, research by the Alliance for Universal Digital Rights and Equality Now found that no definition of doxxing is present in international human rights law and there is no guidance to tackling this problem, despite the severe risks this poses.[17]

One of the reasons that online harassment and digital misogyny still fails to be taken or addressed seriously is because of the mental disconnect we have between what happens online and our offline realities. Harms that happen online, which would be unacceptable offline, are excused because they're seen as just that – solely existing online. But the sexist abuse that unfolds online flows both ways, and it shapes the material world. In 2016, British Labour female politician Jo Cox fell victim to the pervasive impacts of digital harms when she was murdered by Thomas Mair, a man from her constituency whose obsession with far-right ideology was fuelled by what he saw on the internet. This moment should have been a wake-up call for us all – one that finally galvanised us into ending violence against women both online and offline, but sadly women are still not safe today.

Change is slow. The Online Safety Act originally had

no mention of any guidance for keeping women and girls safe online. If it were not for campaigning organisations such as Glitch, the End Violence Against Women Coalition and many more, this would have gone unchanged, but after six years of campaigning, they managed to get an amendment that will hold tech companies to account for women and girls' safety. Seyi Akiwowo founded Glitch, one of the organisations responsible for campaigning for this legislative change. What led her here were her own personal experiences of online misogyny and abuse. At the age of twenty-three, Seyi achieved something monumental. She was elected as the youngest Black female councillor in East London. But when a recording of her went viral for a speech she gave to the European Parliament calling out racism, she was met with the full force of online abuse from strangers online. She used her platform to launch a campaign to 'Fix the Glitch' and subsequently founded Glitch, a non-profit organisation which delivers workshops on digital safety and wellbeing and campaigns for better digital rights for women. It's no wonder that the hypervisibility that women experience offline is translated online, making having something to say render us a target of harassment and vitriol. It seems that many men would prefer if we remain the flattened versions of ourselves that social media algorithms favour – voiceless and passive.

A term that has been raised a lot recently is 'incels', a growing virtual community set on blaming women for their hardships and misfortune. Incels stands for involuntarily celibate, and they are a global online network of men who blame women and the advance of feminism for their inability to establish sexual relationships and intimacy with women. This may sound like some sort of self-pitying support group; however, incel communities are a widely violent and extremist community.

The Center for Countering Digital Hate found that, on average, rape comments were published to an incel forum every thirty minutes.[18] On incel forums almost 1,000[19] references to misogyny and violent action are recorded daily, with these coming to life in attacks such as in 2020 in Toronto when a seventeen-year-old boy entered a massage parlour and killed receptionist Ashley Arzaga, using a machete engraved with the words 'thot slayer' (thot being a degrading slur standing for That Ho Over There). He admitted to being inspired by misogynist incel ideology online and other incel killers. In his pocket was a note that read 'Long Live the Incel Rebellion'.[20] Worryingly, there is a growing interest in mass murders on incel sites, with posts mentioning incel mass murders increasing by 59 per cent between 2021 and 2022.[21]

Already, there have been multiple terrorism attacks where men have killed innocent people in the name of their incel ideology, including the Isla Vista attacks in 2014 where 22-year-old Elliot Rodger shot six people and injured fourteen more before shooting himself dead after posting a misogynistic manifesto online, and the Plymouth shootings which left five people dead. Despite the wave of violence unfolding, of all the incel-related attacks across the globe, only one has been termed a terrorism offence.[22] Maggie Blyth, who is the National Police Lead for Violence against Women and Girls, says that influencers like Andrew Tate are fuelling the radicalisation of young men and boys, and that counter-terrorism police are working to prevent this in order to tackle violence against women and girls.[23]

It's clear that incel violence and ideology still isn't being taken seriously, arguably because of its digital and antifeminist roots. In the UK, Counter Terrorism Policing warned that there was a growing rise in the number of boys and young men becoming referred to Prevent (the government's counter-terrorism strategy) under the category 'mixed, unstable or unclear'. This category was the most popular ideology that boys and young men were being referred under, followed by 'Islamist' and then 'right-wing radicalisation'.[24]

Since incels are included in this category, why then is there not an overt category for antifeminist ideology, instead of the ambiguous 'mixed, unstable or unclear'? We see far too often that young white men who commit acts of violence are framed as unstable, or as victims of their own outbursts, and this limits our ability to tackle these problems at the root, and prevent them from happening again. Their violence is attributed to poor mental health, rather than having ideological roots.

Instead of viewing incel violence as alien or fleeting, we must tackle its growth as a symptom of a wider politics of digital misogyny, which is creating a growing risk of violence. The recognition of extreme misogyny as a form of extremism by the Labour government in 2024 was a step towards tackling the impact that online radicalisation is having on the lives of women and girls offline, but as long as social media's addictive algorithms continue to spread inflammatory and hateful content, extremism in all forms will remain epidemic.

In her book *Collapse Feminism*, YouTube essayist Alice Cappelle writes about how people become vulnerable to forms of radicalisation as a result of the social media content pipeline, and nowhere is this more apparent than in the rise of misogyny and sexist beliefs among young boys and men. Due to the way that our feeds are an assortment of content that our algorithms suspect we will engage with (like, watch or share), we are constantly being exposed to content that we are predicted to be interested in. While young men might not be seeking out this content by choice, algorithms push them towards it. Research entitled 'The Rise of the Aggro-rithm' by Vodafone found that 69 per cent of boys aged between eleven and fourteen have been exposed to online content that promotes misogyny and other harmful views.[25] Until you lose a loved one to the radicalisation process, you don't realise just how pervasive its impacts can be, and how this is tearing relationships apart. In an article for *Hyphen*, a Muslim woman shared her experience of her boyfriend being radicalised into incel content online, sharing how he would send her videos with titles like 'WAKE UP: FREE YOURSELF FROM THE MATRIX' and 'HOW FEMINISM DESTROYS WOMANHOOD'. Online in the 'manosphere', this process of radicalisation is also known as 'red-pilling', and is something that is promoted by those engaged in this type of far-right ideology.

Figures like Andrew Tate might get laughs from young men and boys who claim their statements to be banter, but the gradual desensitisation that can result from engaging with casual misogynistic content is a gateway to more extreme radicalisation. At the same time, incel ideology capitalises on men's unhappiness and despair, fuelling cycles of self-deprivation and shame. In her seminal work *Men Who Hate Women*, journalist Laura Bates reveals how the incel community is one of despair, self-hate and degradation, both towards women and men themselves. A survey into incels found that 67.5 per cent of incels had considered suicide.[26] Suicide in men is generally connected to feelings of inadequacy and shame, generated by not meeting the culturally dominant gender roles, and this feeling of inadequacy is a core pillar of incel ideology.[27] The unrealistic standards of masculinity, ones that flaunt limitless wealth and power that figures like Tate promote, teach young boys and men to see themselves only through their material contributions. Meanwhile, social media platforms and search engines profit from extreme content at the expense of societal harm, putting us at risk by enabling the dissemination of toxic ideologies. It's clear that tackling incel ideology is not only essential for the safety of women, but also for the safety and mental wellbeing of men and boys too.

An undercover investigation by the *New York Times* found that the founders of the suicide forum that took my sister's life were also responsible for founding the world's leading incel forum, a body image forum and an unemployment forum.[28] Concerningly, the only forum of all of these digital spaces that allows women in is the suicide forum.[29] It's no wonder then that incel men who have fantasies of being violent towards women, or seeing women suffer, might use this very suicide forum to seek out a victim – a woman to watch in the depths of her pain and despair.

Roberta Barbos was one of these women. When she was a student at Glasgow University, she was messaged by a man through the forum offering to help her take her life. 'I'm based in Glasgow, and have a hell of a lot of experience with hanging . . . I'd be happy to aid if you want,' he said. Roberta decided to meet Craig McInally at a cafe but soon after cut off communication. Within weeks, prosecutors contacted Roberta to alert her that he had also persuaded two other women from the site to meet, and had then sexually assaulted them and tried to hang them.[30]

The parallels between Roberta's experience and my sister's have forced me to reckon with the possibility that the man who was with my sister when she died, who flew across the world to be there in her most vulnerable moments, had sinister intentions – that he could have sought my sister out when she was at her lowest and preyed on her when she was unwell, living out a sick fantasy as an incel who wants to see a young and vulnerable woman end her life. This is a fear that haunts me and my family, and I can only hope that I am wrong, but given the growing rise of incel ideology and extreme misogyny across the globe, and the sinister origins of the suicide forum that Aimee came to find herself on, I can't help but feel this was not a community designed to support those who need it, but allow twisted men a way of finding them.

There are ways we could alter digital technology so it does not assist abusers or amplify misogyny. By prioritising user safety and prevention over cure, designers and engineers could make sure that their gadgets cannot be weaponised by perpetrators and abusers, preventing harm at the root of the device. Dr Leonie Tanczer, who leads the Gender and Tech research project at University College London, is someone who supports this approach, stating that manufacturers of smart devices ought to consider the needs of victim-survivors as an effective way of preventing further technology-facilitated abuse.[31] Similarly, Hera Hussain, founder of Chayn, emphasises the value in trauma-informed design principles. 'What we need to do is have safety measures in place from the very beginning, rather than implementing them after harms happen.' The architecture of our digital landscape and the tools we use daily is constantly evolving, but it's vital that it evolves with safety at the core. If tech companies were to adopt a safety by design approach, these risks could be alleviated.

Beyond this, content must be moderated, just as it would be in the offline world.

However, the digital abuse that women face today cannot be eradicated with tech solutions alone, such as regulating social media through legislation, making it safe by ending addictive and predatory algorithmic design, and holding social media platforms to account when they fuel violence against women and girls. 'Tech is there to assist us for sure, but it would be futile to tackle this issue without addressing other root causes first,' Yigit Aydinalp, at ESWA (European Sex Workers' Rights Alliance), reminds me. What we need is to end the rife misogyny that breeds violence against women and girls, both offline and online. Freddie Cocker is the founder and editor-in-chief of Vent, an organisation that aims to provide a safe space for men and boys to voice their feelings and struggles. 'My focus the last few years has been on the amount of boys, especially working-class boys, falling behind in education, the lack of positive male role models, including the current dire lack of male teachers in primary school settings. [. . .] If we tackle these problems, as well as give men who have been victims of domestic abuse, sexual abuse or other issues the trust and space to have a voice, we will go a long way to helping men long-term.'

The reactionary movement of antifeminist men that women have been met with online, and the growing political polarisation between young men and women, is a societal challenge that demands collective solutions. From figures like Andrew Tate, boys learn that exploiting and belittling women is big business, and grants you social status. There needs to be more men role-modelling and challenging these notions that to be successful, loved and fulfilled does not mean being against women, but taking strides with them.

CHAPTER 9

Workers, Not Robots

'Workers are not treated as humans but as computational infrastructure.'

Phil Jones[1]

In 1930, British economist John Maynard Keynes made a prediction that would be music to the ears of workers across the globe. He envisioned that future technological developments would reduce our working hours to just a fifteen-hour working week by 2030, giving us more time for leisure, creativity and pleasure. In this alternative reality, technology would not only improve our working lives, but enrich our personal ones too, by granting us more free time. Sadly, his utopian vision was far off the mark. Instead, digital technology in the realm of work has been seized upon to reinforce the same age-old inequalities, consolidate the power of bosses and executives and exploit our labour as workers. Just like women in the digital sphere, workers are dehumanised. Though technological innovation has made our work lives more flexible, it has also given us the gift of more work, not less. Our digital work lives are inseparable from our home lives, and there are more tools than ever before to ensure the lines are blurred. This has led to resistance from workers, like those in France who won the right to disconnect in 2017, giving them the right to ignore work emails outside of working hours. Capitalism and consumerism are pushing the digital sphere to develop and advance so we are labouring, and consuming, more than ever before.

Of course, this isn't to say there haven't been benefits in the process. Just a few decades ago our easy forms of communication didn't exist, including email, which is now what the majority of white-collar workers spend their time doing. Contacting colleagues across the world was immensely costly and long-winded before the internet. Even paying for services, something most of us now do from the comfort of our homes, was something that required a process of going to the bank at a minimum. Telephones and fax machines meant that the workplace was the only place you could work from, and there was no modern understanding of working from home before mobile phones and laptops were introduced.

Today, digital technology is intrinsic to our work lives, whether it's the moment that we find a job vacancy online, to the digital skills we put on our CVs, to networking on LinkedIn, or Teams and Slack being our virtual offices. All of these technologies have made our work lives more efficient, smoother sailing and less clunky. But in making us more efficient, and everything more convenient, they have made the demand of labour higher. They have also divided us in many ways. Remote work – something that is only possible because of recent digital innovation – has eroded the culture of face-to-face community and worker solidarity that many workplaces once had. Working from home has atomised us, granting us convenience while we become detached from our colleagues. Most of us interact with digital algorithms more than we do with our colleagues, and isolation at work has taken on a new meaning, with the Pew Research Center finding remote workers are twice as likely to feel lonely at work compared to office workers.[2]

When I was interviewed for a job using artificial intelligence, I quickly realised just how impersonal our professional lives had rapidly become, if technology is embraced without workers' needs in mind. Facing my reflection on a screen, a ten-second countdown prepared me to answer the questions on the spot. When I didn't get the job, I couldn't help but think if an actual employee had been able to get a sense of my personality, with there being the opportunity for me to ask questions, things might have been different. Did my failure to point score by using keywords in my answers or speak clearly enough for the algorithm to detect cost me the job? Stories like mine are becoming more common, as workers' needs and rights remain the missing puzzle piece of digital trans-formation at work. If an algorithm is going to replace your human boss, profits might be boosted in the short term, but what will this mean for long-term turnover of staff or employee satisfaction? Spying on workers with surveillance might help identify gaps where workers are easing off, but what does this mean for the company culture and worker wellbeing?

The problem here is not the technology itself, it's the motivation behind implementing these tools. So far, most of these new workplace technologies have been implemented under the guise of boosting 'efficiency'. Terms like efficiency and productivity sound great in theory, but more often than not, technologies that boast the ability to make us more efficient just means more work for workers, while bosses accumulate the profits. Instead of only considering efficiency and productivity when we rush to embrace new technologies in the workplace, it should be asked if such advancements will empower workers and users. There are tools that truly help workers do a better job, of course, but there are others that cut corners for those at the top and create new risks of harm for employees. We all understand that artificial intelligence and algorithms are increasingly being implemented into our working lives, but we're yet to know what the future holds and how this will impact the common person. However, there is one thing that is certain: if technologies are implemented without workers' interests at the forefront, we will all lose out.

One worker who understands this is Garfield. A 59-year-old Universal Receive at Amazon's Coventry warehouse, he has been working handling parcels and packages for over five years. In 2023, Garfield and his colleagues made history by being part of the first ever UK Amazon strike. This strike action came after 95 per cent of union members voted to strike, following their long fight for a salary of £15 an hour, which was rejected at the time.[3]

But pay wasn't the only issue that made working at Amazon exhausting for workers like Garfield – it was the growing use of surveillance software that has made workers' lives a misery. Every day Garfield and his colleagues had to use a handheld scanner to monitor individual speed and performance. 'When we executed an action, it registered as being completed, but if our performance spiked in idle time then management would ask us why that happened – though it's often due to system error,' Garfield told me while on strike. 'I have learned to keep an extensive log of where I go and what I do in case I get asked why I've had a spike. Ultimately we get on with it, but it's stressful having to constantly prove that you're not making errors.' Even toilet breaks are enough to get you called into a disciplinary meeting. 'If you have an idle time of an hour total because you go to the loo three times in a ten-hour shift, you'll be penalised for a bodily function,' explained Garfield.

This is not just an invasion of privacy, but a source of serious mental and often physical strain. If you've ever had a micromanager, you understand the overbearing mental toll of feeling like your every move is being constantly analysed and watched. Research from the Institute for the

Future of Work found that the more that workers were exposed to surveillance technology, robotics or software based on AI, the worse their health and wellbeing tended to be.[4] So not only is this type of work culture damaging for a worker's self-esteem and worth, it's physically toxic for workers and puts their health at risk. Garfield himself told me that he could feel his joints seizing up from the endless striving to be working as fast as possible for hours on end, just to avoid disciplinary action.

The worst-case scenarios are horrifying. As Stuart Perry, a regional organiser at GMB (a union with over 500,000 members in the UK), told me for Huck, 'The horror stories you hear are true. We've supported people who have had miscarriages in the toilets, electrocution from poorly maintained equipment, workers being called in for disciplinary action for being off sick with cancer.' The dehumanising impacts of being pushed to physical limits through the use of surveillance technologies that track worker movements and speeds is what Communication Workers Union rep Eugene Caparros calls a 'sociopathic attitude to vulnerable workers'. When technologies are used by employers to extract every last drop of productivity out of their workers, instead of making workers' lives and jobs easier, workers like Garfield suffer the physical and mental consequences. People are not simply productivity machines that have an unfaltering ability to maintain identical levels of performance day in, day out, our bodies and minds have limits. As it stands, technologies are implemented without workers' interests at the forefront, and this is eroding workers' hard-earned rights in the process.

Today, managers often trust tech more than human workers, eroding the employer–employee relationship and creating scarily impersonal working conditions. Ayse is a mum from Turkey, and whilst her daughter is at school she works in a call centre. She works a zero-hour contract, meaning her salary is based on the number of calls she can get through, handling customer service calls for airlines, delivery services and banks. 'We check in and out when on breaks using a system called Spark. If we are one minute late, the system alerts our manager, who immediately messages us to ask why we haven't got back to work,' she told me. 'Through Spark, our managers monitor how long we spend on a customer call. We have targets of twenty minutes to close each customer call. If we go over twenty minutes, our managers start sending us 'whispers', which are messages telling us to hurry up and cut the call.' Not only does this disrupt her when she is often in the middle of closing customer deals, it makes for really stressful working conditions, where Ayse and her colleagues are in a constant state of stress and fear.

The technology that makes this possible is bossware. Bossware is a type of surveillance software that allows employers to spy on their workers through their work devices. From tracking keystrokes to sensing pause time to even more intrusive spying like taking photos through a webcam and even heat sensors under desks, employers are seizing every opportunity to work us harder and longer.

As if straight out of an episode of *Black Mirror*, these tools are even being used to analyse workers' tone and speed of voice, word choice and even their emotional states. You may not be aware if you've been spied on at work; however, a growing number of companies are adopting these creepy tools to monitor their workers' every move.

Polling by the Trade Union Congress in 2022 found that 60 per cent of workers say they have experienced technological surveillance at work in the past year.[5] Bossware surveillance became a growing phenomenon during the pandemic, when remote working became the norm and a moral panic around the lack of presenteeism and slacking behaviour spread across employers. Concerningly, this doesn't affect us all equally, and predatory technologies reinforce the same inequalities that previously came from workplace discrimination. An IPPR report found that women, Black workers and young people are all more likely to be surveilled at work.[6]

This is nothing new, for the culture of enforced productivity and surveillance at work is one that has been used to punish and suppress people throughout history. The panopticon is an architectural design of a prison whereby a guard from a central watch tower can observe all prisoners in their cells at all times. Prisoners know they're possibly being watched but cannot see the watchman, so have to assume they're being watched at all times. Popularised by French philosopher Michel Foucault in *Discipline and Punish: The Birth of the Prison*, the reason the design of the panopticon is so powerful is less about the physical conditions but the mental conditions it creates in the person being watched. By establishing the conditions of an 'internalised surveillance', this type of design serves the purpose of social control. The same idea goes for digital surveillance techniques at work today. Workers like Ayse don't know exactly when they're being watched, so behave as though they constantly are. 'It's a real culture of fear that tries to drive performance through this veil of productivity,' says Stuart Richards, a regional organiser for GMB.

Bosses aren't only using emerging technologies to spy on workers, they're using them to make vital decisions about them too. From determining your compatibility for a potential role before you're hired, to evaluating your performance at work, to deciding whether to sack you, decisions that we assume are made by human managers are being left to the calculations of algorithms. You might have used ChatGPT to write your cover letter thinking you're a step ahead of the game, but you'd be wrong. Employers are ten steps ahead, and they're using algorithms and artificial intelligence to assess CVs, interview candidates, and even hire and fire.

Algorithmic management is the process by which bosses manage, track and analyse workers using algorithms. It's a growing concern for trade unions because it has the risk of subjecting workers to unfair and unlawful decision-making. In the UK and the US, a growing number of employers have taken steps towards diversity and inclusion, particularly in the wake of the Black Lives

Matter movement which gained immense momentum in 2020 after the police killing of George Floyd. From DEI (Diversity, Equity and Inclusion) policies to affirmative action schemes that focus on hiring under-represented groups, there are great strides being made. But sadly, the use of algorithmic decision-making is wreaking havoc and creating further opportunities for discriminatory practices at work to re-emerge. Colin Davidson, senior associate in employment and discrimination law, believes that these tools might instead reverse the societal progress we've made in tackling inequalities in the workplace. 'This could give rise to discriminatory bias with regards to candidates with a disability or neurodiversity who might have difficulties interacting or responding to the AI prompts, or themselves being understood by AI.' Uber is one company whose discriminatory algorithmic management has led to marginalised workers wrongly losing their livelihoods. In 2021, the Independent Workers' Union of Great Britain took Uber to court over its facial recognition algorithm, which is five times more likely to terminate darker-skinned workers' accounts, leaving workers without their livelihoods in an instant.[7]

An inflated sense of trust in technology rather than in workers puts us in a vulnerable position, and a lack of accountability of companies has catastrophic consequences. The most infamous case that encompasses the dangers of trusting technology is the Post Office scandal, the biggest automation project in Europe at the time, which has become the most widespread miscarriage of justice the Criminal Cases Review Commission has ever seen. Around 3,500 sub-postmasters were wrongly accused and more than 900 were wrongly prosecuted for theft and false accounting after errors in the Fujitsu IT system made it look like they were stealing money.[8] This ruined careers, tarnished reputations, tore apart communities, bankrupted families and even caused the suicide of at least one former sub-postmaster. The impacts of the technological flaw were catastrophic, but this wasn't just the fault of a glitch. This was the consequence of a misplaced trust and faith in computer judgements instead of workers, who were making the problems known from the beginning.

When technology is assumed to be objective and incapable of error, workers lose out. Horizon was the software responsible, and was the single biggest automation project in Western Europe when installed. 'It was too big to fail in the eyes of the authorities,' says Andy Furey, national officer for sub-postmasters at the Communication Workers Union, which supports more than 300 sub-postmasters. Recovering the human lens that is the foundation of our workplace relationships in the digital age could not be more urgent, at a time when techno-solutionism reigns.

One form of work that has been made possible in the digital age is the gig worker. The poster child of digital transformation, gig workers are independent contractors who engage in temporary or freelance work on an informal or in-demand basis. This industry is often touted as the success story of a world of work ruled by technological innovation, with Uber, Deliveroo, Just Eat, Lyft and Fiverr becoming household brands who offer quick and convenient services to people based on their network of gig workers. It's near impossible to imagine a world now without the gig economy, and if you have ever ordered Deliveroo or Just Eat to your home or taken an Uber, then you have been playing an integral part in it. The Trades Union Congress reports that 4.4 million people in the UK work in the gig economy at least once a week.[9] The gig economy and its pioneers have marketed themselves as the epitome of freedom and flexibility and, to an extent, this is true. In the gig economy, digital platforms earn their profits by taking a commission on transactions between a service provider and a customer. Gig workers – like Uber drivers and Deliveroo riders – don't have an office and they work using an app on their phones. They don't have the same constraints of being tied down to set hours or having to report to a manager.

But what they have instead isn't freedom, it's exploitation, and the digital platforms that pay these workers make that exploitation possible. Most gig workers are not classified as employees or workers, but as independent or self-employed. What this means is the companies they work for can evade the duties and responsibilities that an employer would normally have to their workers such as sick pay, maternity pay and pensions. Being classified as an employee is a right that we often take for granted, but it is important as it is a legal status that earns you rights that an employer must oblige by, and these are rights that workers throughout history fought relentlessly to win. Corporations in the gig economy profit from the active disenfranchisement of gig workers and technological advancement is eroding fundamental worker rights. Through the very framework of hyper-flexibility, these digital platforms establish an exploitative power relationship with their workers, where the companies that pay them owe them less than the bare minimum.

Uber is one company that has seized this technical distinction between employees and independent contractors to squeeze as much labour out of its drivers as possible. As labour correspondent Polly Smythe writes, since 2009 'the ride-share giant has slashed the per mile bonus for those driving electric vehicles from 15p to 3p, cut drivers' commission from customer fares by 5 per cent, and reduced the pay rate to the fixed price of £1.25 per mile.[10] What this means for workers is an unpredictable income and an unstable livelihood. Many Uber drivers report having to sleep in their vehicles when not on shift and are subject to unpaid waiting time between jobs. I once booked an Uber from my home and when I got in the car, my driver pleaded with me to use my toilet before we started our journey telling me that he had not been in over nine hours. When a worker has to constantly be on the clock competing with other drivers, to the point where they do not have time to use the toilet in order to earn a decent wage, we ought to ask ourselves if this is really a sign of an innovative future or a regression to a bleak past?

In the twenty-first century, it's about time we established an employer–worker relationship that is empowering and collaborative, as opposed to extractive. As workers, wherever we work and whatever we do, we must have a voice in shaping the decisions that will determine the future of our working lives. In fact, 69 per cent of working adults in the UK think employers should consult their staff before introducing new technologies such as AI in the workplace.[11] New technologies should be designed and utilised to make our work lives less strenuous, with the voices and desires of workers at the heart of them.

Knowing how your data is being used at work is a key step to protecting and asserting your rights at work. Jeni Tennison OBE is the founder and executive director of Connected by Data, an organisation that aims to ensure communities have a say in decisions made with and about their data. She believes that workers are a key community who currently experience a power imbalance, and this is driving the unfair use of data-driven technologies. If workers had a genuine say in shaping the adoption and use of these tools, our jobs would only be made easier. 'Employers need to engage and negotiate with workers to prioritise what problems technology is brought in to address; listen to them to understand its impact; and ensure workers can challenge decisions that affect their work and opportunities,' says Jeni. Currently, UK GDPR legislation is a valuable tool for workers to know what AI their employer is using in relation to them, but sharing information with colleagues is an essential way to gather information about your working conditions.

In 2015, former gig worker James Farrar took Uber to court for breaking UK employment law by failing to offer basic worker rights, including national minimum wage and holiday pay.[12] One of the main tools that Uber seized on in an attempt to discredit James's case during the employment tribunal was his data. 'Uber came to court with sheets of my personal data, my work data. Infographics on how I worked, when I worked, where I worked, what I earned, and this was data I had no access to, yet here it was in a bundle and they were trying to use it against me.'

But this didn't deter him, despite how intimidating the experience was. By making subject access requests to collect his data as a worker, he used this to take legal action against Uber for the active misclassification of workers as self-employed. James made history when he achieved a landmark Supreme Court ruling in 2021 declaring that Uber drivers must be treated as workers, rather than self-employed, with this distinction giving them significant employment rights. The case led to settlements to more than 70,000 Uber drivers, resulting in a payout total of around £465 million.[13] James's case led him to found the Worker Info Exchange, a non-profit organisation dedicated to empowering workers to gain insight and access to the data collected from them at work. Sharing data amongst workers has always been a tool for fighting for change at work, whether we realise it or not. If you've ever talked to your colleagues about your salary or workload, that's an act of data exchange, and it's one that's extremely useful for noticing patterns of unfairness, discrimination and salary discrepancies.

Fairwork is another example of how workers can reclaim their data to fight for better working conditions. Founded by Mark Graham, researcher at the Oxford Internet Institute, after years of researching platform work, Fairwork allows workers to score platforms they've worked for on how fairly and ethically they treat workers. By comparing those scores on public league tables, this data incentivises platforms to improve working conditions, a pressure that the monopolistic nature of the gig economy has historically avoided. So far, this has resulted in sixty-six changes in fair management, twenty-one changes in fair pay and forty-one changes in fair conditions.[14]

If you've never experienced algorithmic management or surveillance in your workplace, you might think that you're excluded from the ways that technology is being used to extract more labour from us with no reward. But you'd be mistaken. With the rise of generative AI, the extraction of unpaid labour at the core of the Big Tech business model has multiplied at relentless speed. Many of us have now experimented with generative AI, be it asking ChatGPT to write an email for you or having an artsy avatar version of yourself created using Midjourney. Whilst the ability of a software to take a prompt and create something substantial out of it from thin air might seem magical, the reality is that this work comes from somewhere, and it's closer to you than you might think.

Generative AI works by stealing: by scraping from the vast collection of content that is available online – be it our tweets, profile photos, forum conversations, news articles – and remixing it. Generative AI tools create stuff that looks somewhat original, with no credit or compensation to those whose content helped make it. This is the process of machine learning, where artificial intelligence is taught how to do something using existing inputs and data. But due to the black box AI system that generative AI uses, nobody quite knows what inputs are going into the system, making this type of content theft almost impossible to pin down. This enabled theft is one of the main reasons that the generative AI space race is unfolding at a speed incomparable to things we've seen before. Because unlike other industries that are regulated and have corporate responsibility frameworks in place for what is ethical and fair, tech companies are being allowed to steal to make their fortunes. The manic scramble for AI dominance between companies like DeepMind, Anthropic and OpenAI is a battle for the monopoly over the industry's next best thing.

Here is an example of the double standards that tech companies are being granted. When writing a book, if you want to quote a book, film, song or almost anything, you have to seek copyright permission (which is basically legal consent) and in some cases pay a fee. When tech companies like OpenAI and DeepMind create generative AI products, they steal our digital content to train their tools, be it the blogs and captions we wrote, the voice notes we sent to a friend, the photos we posted, or the emails we've exchanged without our permission. In 2024, Meta announced they would be using everything that Instagram and Facebook users have posted publicly to train their artificial intelligence model, with only EU and UK users being given the option to opt out thanks to data privacy laws.[15] LinkedIn did the same, opting all users into training their generative AI models in September 2024, unless users opt out. What's more, once their product is raking in the millions and soon billions, we get none of the compensation for our content that made these very tools' existence possible. The tech industry's exploitation of our unpaid labour has to end, and if there wasn't already an argument strong enough for this, let generative AI be it.

Many who work in the tech industry are having to make the hard choice between their careers and their moral values, because of the debates around access and ownership unfolding at the heart of generative AI. Ed Newton-Rex was former head of studio at Stability AI, and has worked in AI and music for thirteen years. He resigned from the company over the ethics of using creative work and copyright content to develop AI without consent, an issue which it is facing legal action for.[16] For creative professionals, generative AI poses terrifying risks for the future of our livelihoods. In 2023, authors such as Margaret Atwood and Jodi Picoult signed an open letter from The Authors Guild urging that tech companies responsible for generative AI software stop using their works without authorisation and compensation.[17] There have also already been legal cases from renowned talent like *Game of Thrones* author George R R Martin and John Grisham against tech companies over generative AI and the use of copyrighted works. Already, we can see the urgent need for regulation that protects us from these technologies and the harms that could arise from them if left unattended.

The internet has long been a place where artists and creatives alike can come to share their work without traditional barriers to the arts that persist offline. If you are an emerging creative, you will have been told that the first thing you can do to pursue your creative path is create a social media profile to get your work out there. The evolution of digital technologies has been fundamental to many of our crafts, making it possible to create new things and experiment with new mediums, be it Photoshop or GarageBand. But the tech corporations who have created generative AI tools are now taking advantage of that creativity, and artists are being forced to make decisions about whether to lose out on the community and opportunities that come from sharing online, or risk having their work stolen.

Recognising the dizzying dilemma that generative AI presents for creative fields, many artists and writers are already speaking out against the software. Artists have organised digital protests, with users on sharing platform ArtStation posting images of a stop sign with the caption 'NO TO AI GENERATED IMAGES' over their portfolios.[18] Art and creativity sit uniquely in the AI debate, since many of us recognise that art is inherently human, and that to outsource this process of creation to robots would be mimicry at best, and mockery in most cases. Here again, the same cycle repeats itself: Big Tech extract and profit, while we lose out. Resisting these forms of extraction is not only a fight against exploitation, it is a fight to preserve creativity itself.

In the nineteenth century, a movement of resistance sparked in Britain's textile factories. New machinery was being introduced into cotton and woollen mills by bosses to drive down costs and replace skilled labourers. Textile workers were concerned with how these machines could put their jobs at risk, and resolved to take action. Groups of workers began destroying the machines, across Nottinghamshire, Yorkshire and Lancashire, and eventually the military were called upon to suppress the resistance, with many being executed for their struggle. The Luddites were born out of the belief that technology at work should not be adopted if it means threatening worker status and job security. There are strong parallels today between the Luddites of the nineteenth century and workers across the world fighting for the fair and consensual implementation of technology at work today.

Hollywood has long been known for its glamour and lure of possibility. It oozes individuality, the idea that you can climb your way to the top based on pure hard work and talent. Rarely do we associate it with the advancement of workers' rights. But in 2023, that changed. The union that represents actors and media workers, SAG-AFTRA, saw their biggest vote to strike in the union's history. The issue at stake? Artificial intelligence. The same year that ChatGPT captivated the world's attention, with millions of us rushing to create an account in awe at generative AI's capabilities, some of the world's most talented actors and screenwriters stopped us in our tracks.

Following one of the longest labour strikes in Hollywood, history was made. The Writers Guild of America won new terms of agreement over the use of generative AI, meaning that studios cannot use AI to write scripts, edit scripts written by a writer, or use generative AI to source material and then ask writers to adapt it.[19] The rise of automation and the adoption of new technologies in the workplace was and always has been a threat to job security and worker autonomy. Whereas back then it was mechanised looms, today it's artificial intelligence – not because workers are against technology, but because technologies are being used to extract more value from workers without them being paid for it.

Unions across the globe have always been on the front line of fighting back against the exploitative use of technology at work, and today, with the growing use of artificial intelligence and algorithms at work, that has taken on a new level of importance. The Trades Union Congress, which consists of forty-eight unions and was founded in 1868; has long fought for workers' rights and amplified their voices. In 2024, it launched its AI Bill which, if passed, will become the first piece of legislation that protects workers from the risks and harms of AI-powered decision-making at work, closing the gaps that currently exist in UK law. 'Through collective bargaining, unions and workers have an important role to play in the governance of technology at work, with collective agreements putting in place consultation systems, protections, rights and obligations to ensure the fair and effective use of new technology,' Mary Towers tells me. 'Collectivism is even more important at a time when, through technology, only one set of interests is currently being represented.'

There is immense potential for technology to make workers' lives easier, but what we are seeing become clear is that this can only happen if digital technology is implemented with workers' rights and needs in mind. It might sound utopian, but imagine a workplace where we were consulted on what technology might actually help us do our jobs better, or even give us more time to do the things that we love outside of work. Think tank Autonomy published a paper which looked into how AI might give us more free time if these tools were used for our collective good. The paper found that by 2033, 88 per cent of the labour market in Great Britain could have working hours reduced by at least 10 per cent, if AI was introduced into workplaces with the goal of creating free time for workers.[20] That is the type of technological innovation we need to be aiming for, but it won't be given to us without a fight. So much of our work, whatever field we are in, has human relationships at the core of what we do and no technology – no matter how time- or cost-saving – is equipped to replace that.

CHAPTER 10

I Post, Therefore I Am

'We were all self-centred together, supporting each other as we propped up the social media companies.'

Lauren Oyler, *Fake Accounts*[1]

Content is a puzzling phenomenon. It can turn the most mundane experience into a cinematic masterpiece, or a normal day into an intimate insight into a stranger's life that you would otherwise never have known. Content creation has always come naturally to me, and been a core part of my life. I still remember clearly the day I lined up my nail polish bottle collection like ducks in a row and painted my index finger, took a photo, removed the varnish and on to the next. The result was a ninety-second stop motion video of my twelve-year-old finger painted an array of colours, moving to the beat of 'Something Good Can Work' by Two Door Cinema Club, titled '50 Shades of Varnish'.

When I was thirteen, becoming a YouTuber was quite possibly the most iconic thing you could ever do with your life, so of course I started a YouTube channel. Today this has moved across to the TikTok platform, where teenagers spend hours creating TikTok content today in the hopes of becoming TikTok famous. I have grown up online and have been immersed in the culture of sharing throughout my day – what I'm eating, where I'm going, who I am with, what I wear and listen to. I've documented every significant life event, from winning rowing races as a teenager, going to prom with my best mate Finn, passing my A levels and getting a place on my dream university course in my favourite city, volunteering abroad, landing my first book deal, my partner and I moving in together. For the past ten years, I've spent hours creating mini content drafts in my mind that I plan to post later, the right clips of events, the right angles capturing my interactions, the outfit that will portray the right image, the lighting that will invoke the right mood, the gestures I'll use to demonstrate the right feelings. Sitting across from my boyfriend on a date, I'll be envisaging my Instagram post later; planning a girls' holiday, I'll be bookmarking TikTok templates I want to make when there; after getting a new career opportunity I'll map out the best way to announce it on LinkedIn.

We've become the directors, actors and scriptwriters of our own lives. Many of us place more value on the content we create of something we've done or somewhere we've been than the thing itself. This is why journalist and author Jia Tolentino argues that online, the representation of things is more valuable than the thing itself – from representation of political action, of happiness, of body confidence, of friendship, of success.[2] We are incentivised to post because there's always another bit of content you could be creating that could be praised or commoditised. Online, we exist either as consumers or creators of content – or both. Our lives are reduced purely to the relationships we have with what makes up the feeds we scroll. In *How To Do Nothing*, Jenny Odell writes: 'In a situation where every waking moment has become pertinent to our making a living, and when we submit even our leisure for numerical evaluation via likes on Facebook and Instagram, constantly checking on its performance like one checks a stock, monitoring the ongoing development of our personal brand.'[3] This is not solely due to the economic pull factor of our digital economy, but our very impulses and desires are being viewed through a commercial prism and forced to fit into the digital architecture of the social media platforms we engage with.

Creating content is now sold to us as a way to secure our future, especially in a world where blowing up on social media can change our lives in unrecognisable ways. Today, for most young professionals and people starting any new venture, the advice is the same: build a profile, build a following, build a brand. In order to network and achieve our aspirations, whether you're a female founder, a DJ, a freelance journalist or aspiring comedian, you have to be not only present and available online, but constantly visible. This is a huge source of pressure for most young people I know, and for many it has become a chore or an (unpaid) job to be on social media. Being current, offering hot takes and knowing what's trending are part of the job – not to mention the endless copywriting, photography, videography, marketing and PR involved too. My career as a journalist has grown alongside the rise of TikTok, and I grapple daily with the unpaid labour involved in constant self-promotion as a means of securing future job opportunities. Some have seen this shift as an indication that we are becoming sell-outs or even shallow in our desire for success, but it's undeniable that learning to be a content creator is now a necessary evil that comes with being a creative in the twenty-first century.

As a freelance journalist I have trained myself almost unconsciously to constantly market myself and my work, creating posts in four different formats for each platform I use, drafting and editing captions and visuals or videos. After writing this book, I was required and encouraged by my publishing team and agent to be as visible as possible, posting consistently in order to galvanise my audience and sell the book. Most creatives are more than aware that in the attention economy, having followers has become another indicator of your ability to build an audience and online community – which are essential to 'making it' as a content creator today. The same way that employers judge your education and qualifications, our followers and like counts are now a reflection of our capabilities and for creatives today are one of the most important tools you can have in your arsenal.

As journalist Rebecca Jennings writes: 'Under the tyranny of algorithmic media distribution, artists, authors – anyone whose work concerns itself with what it means to be human – now have to be entrepreneurs, too.' Industry professionals know and accept this bleak reality. Back in 2022, when I attended an internship interview at *Dazed* magazine, we got to hear from each editor in the team about their experiences of working in the journalism industry. It was an exciting opportunity and like nothing I'd experienced as a freelance journalist before. I'd never met any full-time journalists before so I was intrigued to hear of the industry secrets they might reveal. But the main message they all shared on how to make it in the industry was that you had to be constantly online. It is for this reason that author Taylor Lorenz argues that we are all content creators, whether we consciously choose to be or not.[4]

I didn't realise the driving force that posting content online had over my life until I came to write this book, something that has been a dream of mine since I was a child. As a kid I spent hours with my nose in Jacqueline Wilson books in my bedroom, always loved dressing up for World Book Day and was practically raised in my local library. So when I got a book deal, it was the proudest moment of my life. As a freelance journalist you often feel you're fighting to prove yourself and your abilities in order to pay the bills, so I couldn't wait to publicly share that I would have my first book published with a mainstream UK publisher. But until I started writing it, I had never had to grapple with my own relationship of making my life into content, and what motivates me to do it.

Until you write a book, you never realise how much of the process unfolds in the undocumented moments of your life. The ideas that come to you in the bathroom, staring into space on the bus, listening to your loved ones in a conversation, in between being awake and falling asleep, walking your dogs. It isn't as glamorous as the job title of author will have it seem. At times I felt frustrated (a very privileged frustration to have, I realise) that I had nothing to show for this creative journey, other than a picture of my laptop on my desk, sitting in a dressing gown with my unwashed hair scraped into a bun. My book-writing process felt invisible because only I knew about it. What this meant was that at times I internalised this to mean that this experience and process was unimportant, irrelevant, forgotten.

The reason for this feeling was that there was no spectator, something that social media has programmed us to feel is an essential part of life. The pressure to make this process into something romantic, to be shared and praised online, was something I couldn't shut off, a constant dilemma ringing in my mind that would pull my attention away from writing. This was despite the fact I was juggling writing this book alongside working three days a week as a press officer for Oxfam, grieving and campaigning, pitching and writing articles, all while trying to maintain a social life and look after my mind and body. I thought that simply making more content out of my life would ease the burden of not ever feeling that I was doing enough. Without an audience, I felt invalidated, and it forced me to reckon with the intricate relationship that many of us have come to have with posting online and the digital validation we receive as a result.

These tensions may sound like the traits of a self-obsessed person, but the reality is that they have evolved out of the content culture that rules our world today. In the digital age, visibility and value go hand in hand. 'The Facebook Eye' is a term that was coined in 2012 by Nathan Jurgenson to describe how 'our brains are always looking for a moment where the ephemeral blur of lived experience might best be translated into a Facebook post; one that will draw the most comments and likes.'[5] The validation we seek out online is now the context for so many of our daily interactions, and this is bound to be intensified in our proud moments or the anticipated achievement of personal goals. 'We submit our free time to numerical evaluation, interact with algorithmic versions of each other, and build and maintain personal brands,' writes author Jenny Odell.[6] Writing this book has triggered me to re-evaluate my life and ask myself where the external forces of social media have warped my senses and influenced my decisions. It has made me ask myself how growing up online has influenced my sense of self-worth, and whether I document my life for myself or for external validation. Now I find solace in doing things without documenting them at all, knowing that I'm doing them solely for me, not for the reactions or praise they might get in response.

Many of us now feel that conforming to the endless performativity that social media demands no longer feels like a choice, but a fundamental expectation of modern life. This pressure is only alleviated when you choose to spend an extended period of time offline. After just a few days offline for my twenty-fifth birthday with my girlfriends in Cornwall, I felt so much more grounded, I felt sure of who I am, what I value and care for, and how I want to spend my life. This is because living our lives through the eyes of content pulls us away from ourselves and who we really are, since we spend our time either performing for others or getting drawn into the identities of others. Just three days spent fully immersed in the beautiful company of my friends was enough to make me feel more clarity, lighter just knowing I was existing offline and was totally present in my life.

For those for whom content creation is a full-time job, this dilemma can lead to inescapable burnout and exhaustion. A survey of influencers found that almost 80 per cent of respondents suffer from burnout, with 66 per cent saying it impacts their mental health.[7] Some creators are turning to innovative solutions to combat this, but others are quitting altogether. Jordi van den Bussche is a gaming YouTuber based in Amsterdam who has over 15 million subscribers. But in 2023, he decided to replace himself with an AI avatar to tackle his burnout whilst not losing his digital legacy.[8] Unlike content, fleeting and short-lived in nature, our individual impact does not disappear or expire. The impressions you leave on those around you offline is not lost after a refresh of the feed, and it isn't forgotten after twenty-four hours on your page. Recognising this can empower us to develop the courage to step away from something you've become used to not only using, but existing through. When everything becomes reduced to content, every aspect of our life becomes simply a means to an end.

In 2024, I went on my first solo travel trip. Something that I believed would be freeing, transformative and vibrant actually made me feel frantic, emotional and exposed. I shared how I felt on social media, taking a moment to be truly vulnerable on the app. I wasn't alone. Within minutes, men and women messaged me saying they felt similarly and I was reassured, my anxiety relieved. This is one of the beauties of putting out content into the world as it can make you feel less alone in an instant. However, one of the reasons I had felt discontent during this solo break was because I had been subconsciously comparing my own experience to the highlights reels that I had seen online from travel influencers and seasoned travellers.

The images and videos we post online can be an authentic reflection of our lives and characters, but equally they can be a complete misrepresentation because they can only ever be 2D extractions of a human life, and beyond that they are curations, formulated to express what the creator wants to express. Snippets of our experience in a few chosen images or videos can hardly scrape the surface of the complexity of our lived experiences and the vast range of emotions and situations we live through each day. Social media and the way that algorithms funnel what we see online means that the lived experience becomes reduced to a very slim representation of reality.

For Lee Tilghman, former wellness influencer also known as Lee From America, taking a break from Instagram in 2019 was in fact what allowed her to address her health issues, something that her online audience would have had no idea about. She went to treatment for orthorexia, a condition that involves obsession with wellness and eating healthily but can also manifest as disordered eating. When she returned to the platform, she posted a video apologising for her role in promoting diet culture, and has since quit influencing and now runs a newsletter, Offline Time. When we step back from the content cycle we are able to see there is so much more to life, and that those online pressures we've internalised can simply fall away if we let them.

The feed has long been nicknamed a highlights reel, and it's undeniably the best description of our social media landscape. I even felt apprehensive about posting about my solo trip in a way that didn't make it look utopian. 'Will people think I'm ungrateful for saying something negative?' my mind wondered. But something still pulled me to be open and transparent, and I'm so glad I was. Sharing online has a cumulative effect: when you share, people begin to share back. The only way we can make sure that our online experiences begin to reflect our lived ones is if we are more transparent online. It's rare to see people expressing their small losses, daily hindrances and personal battles, but I'm grateful when they do. It's a sigh of relief, a respite from the posed and planned nature of our timelines. If we all posted the shitty days a little more, we might just feel better that our day-to-day lives aren't as curated as others appear. The offline world is beautiful in all its messiness and this is where authenticity is born, not in a profile of our favourite pictures and curated captions.

The contentification of our entire lives has meant that organic and spontaneous conversation and a lack of control over real-life scenarios can become anxiety-inducing experiences instead of being accepted as just part of human nature. I often get invited to PR events and book launches with people I've interacted with for years online, but the anxiety I get about how I'll be perceived compared to how I am online is sometimes enough to put me off altogether. The false sense of security our curated digital profiles give us simultaneously makes us feel discomfort in completely natural and human situations. I do feel that this plays a part in the rising rates of anxiety that younger people are facing since the rise of social media use and smartphone ownership.

Personally, I noticed that my anxiety was much worse in the couple of years after the pandemic, a time in which I spent so much more of my time socialising and communicating online, over text, email and FaceTime. I'm not the first person to say that social media has profoundly changed our social interactions and the relationships we have with each other. In *Algorithmic Intimacy*, Anthony Elliott argues that the digital revolution has brought with it a distancing from the unpredictability of human relationships and intimacy.[9] I've realised gradually that the reason I feel nervous in spontaneous social settings and big groups of new people is because it requires me to release control, the type of control that constructing messages, emails and posts online grants us.

These anxieties extend not just to strangers, but to our most intimate relationships too, leaving many of us unsatisfied and disconnected. On my sister's first birthday after she passed, my parents, boyfriend and I visited Yorkshire Sculpture Park, a place she had always wanted to visit. Throughout the day, my mum received messages of support from loved ones, sending their love to my parents on this difficult day. But for me, who had briefly mentioned our plan to close friends but not posted anything online, I heard nothing. Crucially, for many Gen Z and millennials who grew up online, and even more so generations who've never known a world without smartphones, posting can come to be our primary way of maintaining and being kept in the loop with our friends' lives.

Before losing my sister, I would regularly use my close friends story as a way of updating all my mates of what was going on in my life. Personally, I have a tendency to isolate myself when I'm feeling low and find it difficult to reach out to friends for support, and this only got harder when I lost my sister. Instead of messaging friends and having to vocalise my grief, I would occasionally post photos of happy memories on my close friends story, hoping that this would elicit a response, rather than messaging my loved ones directly to talk about how I was struggling. But what I was often met with was a resounding emptiness. It's not that my friends were ignoring my sadness, it was that the digital interactions that replaced a cup of tea and a chat – a like of a story, a heart emoji, a one-line text – were nowhere near enough to comfort me in this type of pain. But this was no fault of theirs. I had realised that this surface-level intimacy – something I'm reluctant to call connection – has become the default. So many of us think we are socialising, but all we are doing is exchanging digital metrics in the hope they'll fill the void.

What has come as a result is a warped perception of what it is to be a 'good friend', one that stunts the growth of our close relationships. We mistake digital interactions that make us feel good for as long as they take to do as things to measure our friendships' values on. This depersonalisation of our loved ones is not only unhelpful, it's unfair. This is what author Safiya U. Noble calls the pop-up experience, the one that social media platforms have sold us through their constant talk of connection.[10] Shallow and instant engagements of likes, follows, comments and messages have come to replace deeper in-person interactions, with their convenience making them an instantaneous and easy swap. But what my experience of grieving online taught me was that this was an illusion of closeness that never truly delivered on its promise, for all Zuckerberg's faith in social media as the key to connection. Digital interactions from loved ones fell short of the intimacy I craved and the love I needed, leaving me feeling lonelier than ever. Yasmin Elizabeth, the creator of Pick Me Up Inc, explained how: 'We all have the most friends right now yet are the most lonely. Social media has taken away the value of authentic interaction because people are so accessible that we take it for granted.'

Similarly, in the digital age, we can mistakenly assume ill intentions of our loved ones through the distortion of social media, and the impossibility of posts capturing real-world conversation. The always-on nature of social media and proximity of our digital devices to our persons means we assume that access equates to limitless opportunity to 'reach out'. This is promoted by toxic takes on X that 'if they wanted to, they would'. Social media's visibility places the onus on others, rather than making us consider the part we play in reaching out a hand to those we love. This can end up making us feel reluctant to contact a friend when we genuinely miss their company or need their advice. We are dissatisfied with the reality of our relationships yet social media encourages us to constantly seek out more: more followers, more friends, more interactions, but this is not compatible with our capabilities. Dunbar's number is a cognitive theory that suggests our species can only really have 150 stable social relationships, yet so many of us are fruitlessly scrambling to try to maintain digital relationships with more people than we can possibly remember. Inevitably, social media makes us spread ourselves too thin, because it centres quantity over quality, engagement over depth.

I've spent a lot of time thinking about what this means for my friendships, and how it has made me complacent at times, something that is uncomfortable to accept but necessary to recognise. Focusing too much on showing up online but forgetting to be present for our friends in the material world is undoubtedly going to leave us depleted. For our relationships, the digital sphere has a flattening effect, making us perceive people as shallow and replaceable. Social media should be a supplement to our friendships rather than the sole medium through which we experience them. Instead of blame and resentment, committing and giving more of ourselves to our friends beyond the screen could offer us true fulfilment. As I've shifted away from this toxic cost-benefit analysis of my relationships, the surface-level ones have fallen by the wayside, and my small circle of friendships has become deeply fulfilling.

The glaring solution to me has come to be decentring the role that digital metrics play in our views of our lives. One group of people who are particularly good at this – or at least better than my generation – is older people. My dad goes on international motorbike tours with strangers he has only communicated with a handful of times over email with no hesitation. My mum remembers most of her friends' birthdays with ease, and whilst she regularly uses WhatsApp to chat to them, it's mostly used to arrange the in-person catch-ups, rather than being the end in itself.

Meanwhile, I couldn't count the number of times I've had that uncomfortable guilt of forgetting a friend's birthday until after seeing their posts on Instagram, or that helpful Facebook reminder – sorry! Younger generations who have grown up spending our primary connection building years running alongside the emergence and popularisation of platforms like Instagram and Facebook have lost out as a result. Loneliness rates are highest in young adults, with 27 per cent of young adults aged nineteen to twenty-nine reporting feeling very or fairly lonely. Despite the fact that the word lonely often conjures up an (admittedly ageist) picture of an elderly person who lives alone and who isn't able to get out like they used to, in the same study only 17 per cent of people aged sixty-five and older reported feeling lonely.[11] Social media is hardly social at all.

Logging off seems hard and difficult, but when you consider it deeply, it is the opposite. It is about reconnecting with ourselves and our experiences as human beings were supposed to. Not living to post our lives through a commercialised social media lens, not editing and adjusting to make us something we're not. The most beautiful moments you have had online have probably been when you saw something truly honest and relatable, and every post we do has the potential to be that. But some moments can just be yours and yours alone. They can be quiet moments between you and the world around you, or laughs with loved ones, or incredible achievements too. Not everything needs to be shared and we all have the power and control to hold things back. I don't intend to fully log off just yet, but I intend to one day. The experience of writing this book in solitude, away from the noise and buzz of social media, the constant hum of people's achievements and praise from peers, has been a circuit breaker. *Logging Off* (literally) has changed my perception of what is important, and how just because something isn't visible or publicly shared, announced or documented, it doesn't mean it lacks value.

CHAPTER 11

Keep Up or Carry On

'Is it just me or is the infrastructure for existing without a smartphone just slowly disappearing?'
@ilanaslighty on Twitter, 2023[1]

More often than not, when we speak about technology, we speak about it as something that makes us equal members of society, offering people the opportunity to participate freely in a new dimension of our world. We imagine technology as a force that liberates us from the shackles of stagnancy and isolation. We imagine the digital world as something that connects us, echoing the optimistic visions of tech leaders. Technology is the great equaliser, or so we're told. Getting online today undeniably offers a vast wealth of opportunities, from finding work, to staying in touch with friends, to enjoying music and film, to registering to vote or shopping with convenience. But there are those who are being excluded from the digital conversation. Many of these people are not posting or consuming content or feeling the harmful impact of social media that I've covered in this book. Whether they didn't grow up in the all-consuming era of expanding technology or they have been priced out, there is a huge proportion of the global population who are left out, and because of this they are facing harms and inequalities but of a different kind. The digital world functions like a gated community, one where we are falling into two teams, the digital haves and the digital have-nots.

I've seen first-hand the human cost of digital exclusion. When I moved to Lewes, a small town not far from Brighton, with my boyfriend in the early summer of 2022, I fell in love with the community spirit of the area. It was somewhere everyone knew everyone and strangers would smile at you as you walked past. When we got our first community newsletter through our door, we knew we'd chosen somewhere with a completely different energy to what we had been used to, and we were excited to immerse ourselves in it. Absent-mindedly flicking through ads for local businesses and community events coming up, I spotted a notice in the newsletter which read: SMARTPHONE TUITION REQUIRED BY INTELLIGENT PENSIONER. The self-proclaimed 'intelligent' pensioner made me laugh as it's something that most young people would be too embarrassed to call ourselves, even if we thought we were. I appreciated the self-confidence in the ad, but also the humility needed to ask for help with a skill that many of us would consider easy. People forget we were all new to technology once, and I felt compelled to respond. I called the number on the ad and left a message on the landline saying I might be able to help. Within a few days I was sitting in Tony's beige armchair in his ground-floor flat, decorated with books and guitars from his daily trips to the local charity shops, holding his Tesco mobile phone and showing him how to turn it on.

At eighty-seven years old, Tony was a retired man who had made a career for himself in publishing. He took pride in being well read, intelligent and self-sufficient, which is why putting an ad out to ask for help using his phone hadn't come easily to him. However, Tony felt he had waited long enough, as for over a year his phone had been sitting in a box untouched and collecting dust. This was no fault of his own. Just a week after buying his first ever smartphone, he had a fall while walking his dog Kiki and was hospitalised. When he was discharged, his memory had significantly deteriorated, and daily activities took much more effort than before. A year went by, and by the time I responded to his ad, Tony had been paying a monthly contract for over a year for a phone he didn't even know how to turn on. 'I came away with a smartphone but no instructions. I didn't even know how to receive a call or switch it on and off. Every now and then I went back to Tesco to ask if they could show me how to use it, and they did it willingly, but I wasn't receptive,' Tony told me.

In the UK, 5.3 million people still lack essential digital skills for everyday life.[2] Meeting Tony was the first time I had met one of these people and it was the first time that

I witnessed digital exclusion as a tangible reality. Tony was from a generation who were being served the possibilities of technology much later in life, and they were not such easy things to grasp. 'I want to be able to book a holiday or book a concert. I want to be able to do everything that this thing does, but you can't know what's possible until you're shown.'

Frustratingly, digital skills are the one skill that society has come to assume are self-taught. The fact that society is becoming more digital by the day is often heralded as symbolic of social progress and modernity, but without the education and upskilling this shift requires, people will continue to fall through the cracks. Shockingly, a House of Lords report in 2023 stated that by 2030, basic digital skills are set to become the UK's largest skills gap.[3] Seeing Tony, an elderly man who lived alone being unable to have the social life he desired, struggling to contact loved ones who live abroad and being excluded from accessing the wealth of information many of us have at our fingertips, taught me how disempowering the digital skills gap can be.

I couldn't walk away without knowing I had done my best to equip Tony with the skills he needed. We arranged to have weekly, hour-long meetings to get him up to speed on his mobile. Each time, he'd welcome me with a big grin and a cup of tea, offering me dark chocolate from his secret stash. Tony never failed to prepare; when I arrived, he would be armed with his notebook full of questions for the session. Within weeks, Tony had made leaps and bounds of progress. He went from not knowing how to unlock his phone, to sending me photos of his greyhound Kiki on WhatsApp, from being unsure of how to connect with people, to video-calling his stepson in France. I felt an immense sense of pride, and he seemed lighter and happier with each lesson we had.

When I asked Tony what his biggest challenge with using digital technology was, he told me it was fear. 'I was scared. It was the fear of doing something wrong really, or not. Not being as competent as I felt I should be.' Fear is a universal human experience, but when it comes to technology, each of us have our own experiences. While I've never felt scared of using my phone, this type of intimidating overwhelm is a feeling I have had in other situations when I have been afraid to try something new and step out of my comfort zone. It is normal to have a gap in your knowledge, but we can't expect people to close those gaps without the tools. The speed at which our technology is evolving is rapidly at odds with our speed of equipping ourselves and our communities to navigate the digital world. Even as a Gen Z who uses social media every day, I find myself baffled by new TikTok features, clueless compared to friends who are just a few years younger, because with each day that passes there are a whole host of skills required. Combine this relentless speed with political negligence and you've got a toxic combination. If society has no infrastructure for teaching and maintaining our digital skills, we're left to fend for ourselves or lose out.

Today, many older people struggle with smartphones. When my generation grows old, it might be the next AI innovation or new tech. And so it goes on. Elderly people across the UK experience disproportionately higher rates of digital exclusion and have been largely left to fend for themselves in the digital age. If you have an elderly relative, you'll probably know this already. A quick poll on my Instagram asking my followers if they had ever helped an older relative with their tech revealed the scale of this issue: 257 responded yes, compared to just fourteen who said they hadn't. The digital whizzes among us might have even found their questions funny at times, something I'm guilty of when my dad has asked me how to get off video mode on his phone. But digital exclusion isn't something that my generation will be magically exempt from. While we might imagine ourselves as possessing all the necessary knowledge to navigate tech and carry out our essential activities from our phones *right now*, with each move to a more digital society, the cycle repeats itself. Tony taught me that this isn't down to an unwillingness to learn or adapt – far from it – but a result of societal change unfolding at a rate that many cannot keep up with, and a failure from decision-makers to bridge these gaps with the funding and digital skills education initiatives we so need.

So far, it's been largely left to charities to fill the digital skills gap. Enter Nick, a proud northerner in his sixties, dad of four and Manchester United fan. Working in retail for the past sixteen years he was able to pick up the basic digital skills he needed for his job, but at home he never needed to until four years ago when he came out of work. Since 2022, Nick has been attending weekly upskilling sessions with Starting Point, a Stockport community partnership that helps people learn digital skills. These sessions have enabled Nick to learn how to do things like his banking and bills online, something that has become a norm for millions of people across the UK. It is an essential space for him. 'Everything I do now that is important, whether it's my banking, or paying my gas bill and electricity bill, or getting a doctor's appointment, it's all in my calendar on my phone. If it switched off tomorrow, I'd like to think I could manage without it but I don't think I could.' Today, most of our essential, social and civic activities require us to get online in some way. Having the digital skills to do so can mean the difference between living well and struggling to get through each day. 'Just last week I was trying to get a tax rebate at home using my data, but it kept timing out and it was really frustrating me. I took my phone to a session with Starting Point the next day and within ten minutes I had done it.'

It is great that there are those willing to teach the skills; however, digital inclusion also requires risk awareness. This is a digital literacy skill that is often neglected and framed as an individual responsibility. Just recently, my dad, who started his career in computing before the internet even existed and who has been involved in the digital revolution at every step of the way, came to proudly tell me that the lead guitarist of the Foo Fighters had liked one of his Facebook statuses (yes, really). What I thought was glaringly obviously a fan page, was to my dad a famous person's real profile. Luckily, this was just a like of a post; however, there is a huge problem online where people are impersonating celebrities to commit fraud, using nefarious and clever methods to seek out the vulnerable and scam them. Such accounts will convince the vulnerable person that they are their soulmate, or they are simply a loyal friend. Other times, accounts will pose as a grandchild in distress claiming they need money.

For example, in 2023, Martin Lewis, beloved financial expert, was the victim of a deepfake video that showed an altered version of himself advising people to invest in an opportunity that was fraudulent,[4] and in 2024 a pensioner was scammed out of £13,000 by a fraudster impersonating Tom Jones. This issue is so prolific that nearly three in five (61 per cent) of older people have been a target of financial fraud.[5] Scam awareness and an understanding of risk is essential for vulnerable people to be able to identify the accounts that are targeting them for financial extortion. And while they target the vulnerable, this doesn't mean victims are unintelligent or unaware. These technologies are only becoming more sophisticated, making risk awareness even more challenging.

Increasing digital skills has to happen in tandem with building awareness of the risks. Digital literacy encompasses a whole range of skills needed to use the internet both efficiently and safely. For people who can get online but lack essential online safety skills and cybersecurity knowledge, a whole host of misinformation, fraud or virus risks open to them. During the pandemic, scammers played on people's desperation, sending out scam texts pretending to be sent by the government, offering a false payment in relation to coronavirus support. In the UK, victims lost £1.3 billion in 2021 amid a surge in online fraud, with the amount lost to romance scams soaring by 73 per cent that year.[6] I would often hear from my mum when she worked as a social worker about her frustration and anger at fraudsters who target mentally unwell older people and those with disabilities, taking advantage of their isolation and vulnerability.

Yet, despite the scale of the problem, the UK government's Essential Digital Skills Framework, which aims to outline the essential digital skills needed by everyone in the UK, doesn't mention scams or fraud once.[7] Viewing digital skills as the individual's responsibility, rather than an essential aspect of universal education that ought to be provided by governments within our schools and communities, fuels digital exclusion and compounds existing challenges we face. It's vital, now more than ever, that decision-makers recognise digital skills as an essential right, and a fundamental aspect of basic education.

One mayor leading the way to ensuring that all members of his community have the digital skills and tools to get online is Andy Burnham. Following his re-election in 2021, he announced plans to ensure Greater Manchester would be one of the first cities globally to equip all under-25s, over-75s and disabled people with what they need to get online.[8] The creation of their Digital Inclusion Action Network alongside the Digital Inclusion Taskforce of over 250 actors in industry, public sector, local government, schools and health is an example of a community-led approach to digital transformation that doesn't leave anyone behind.

The trend to moving everything online was exacerbated during the Covid-19 pandemic, when social distancing measures and national lockdowns led to the closure of most businesses and services, with the digital alternatives being an essential replacement. Zoom calls replaced family gatherings and meetings, online shopping became the norm, vital welfare and support services had to be accessed online. As Professor Daniel Miller says, 'The smartphone is no longer just a device we use, it's become the place where we live.'[9] But for those who do not have the digital know-how, or even the tools, this supposedly innocent business decision has rapidly opened up a chasm of exclusion. There are those being left out of the conversation in the mission for progress and technological advancement.

Our general practices are community spaces that have been increasingly moving online. One day, when Caroline from Glasgow noticed a worrying growth on her stomach, she didn't hesitate to call her doctor. She hoped to be seen urgently and thought her doctor would suggest exactly that. But when her doctor told her to email him a photo of the growth, she was left feeling helpless in a health crisis. 'I've got a Nokia. I've no camera because of the simple fact I've got eye problems, and this is easier for me to use.' Thankfully, she has a daughter who was able to come over to take a photo of the growth and send it to her doctor, which led to an appointment and consequently surgery to remove it. But for what turned out to be a life-threatening growth, not owning a smartphone could have been a matter of life or death for Caroline. What if she hadn't had a family member living locally? Would not owning a smartphone be the determining factor of her being able to access vital healthcare?

The relentless replacement of in-person services with online alternatives and the simultaneous failure to close the digital skills gap is the equivalent of building a beautiful city, which boasts brilliant social housing, thriving schools and hospitals, vast public parks and green spaces, but having no transport links or roads built to get to it. How can we enjoy the benefits if we are enabling people to be locked out? Before the pandemic, 66 per cent of all adults had never used the internet or apps to manage their health.[10] But for those without smartphones, laptops or broadband, the digitisation of essential services can mean the difference between good and ill health, with 83 per cent of GPs expressing concern about patients whose access to remote services might be impacted by digital literacy, disability, language, location or internet connection.[11]

Beyond this, there is also an unspoken culture of assuming that everyone can afford digital technology, and has the means to get online. Assuming that everyone can just ping over an email or WhatsApp a photo only stigmatises those who cannot, and makes it harder for those without to engage in society fairly. 'The amount of people that say we'll send you a voucher on your phone, we'll email you on your phone and then you've got to explain that you haven't got that on your phone. And it stigmatises you. You don't want to say you're in poverty so I just say, "Oh, well, I can't use it with my eyes,"' Caroline tells me.

The current failure to make non-digital alternatives available means that disabled people like Caroline are being locked out of accessing vital services. But Caroline is someone who isn't afraid to speak out. She is involved in multiple forums for people who live in poverty to share their experiences and build solutions, including the Poverty Truth Commission, The APLE Collective and Nourish Scotland. 'There's not much that is right with me but my voice is great, so if I can I use it . . .' One huge win that Caroline has managed to achieve was the introduction of NHS 111 services in Scotland, something which came from the combination of her voicing her barriers to access and the newly acquired digital skills she learned during lockdown. She often needs to seek vital health advice, but noticed that calling the NHS service in Scotland, NHS 24, was costing her eight to ten pounds a time. She started an e-petition, and five years on, the free telephone service for health advice was introduced in Scotland. This is what makes working on solutions with those who are directly affected by digital barriers so important, because they are most equipped to propose solutions. As Meredith Broussard writes, 'We achieve remarkable innovation when we open up the pool of people who participate.'[12]

It's increasingly clear that the digital by default methods of service provision we have seen boom in recent years are leaving people with digital barriers to essential services, and this is creating new forms of inequality in today's modern world. Malathy Muthu is the CEO of Skills Enterprise, an organisation in East London that supports people with welfare access and digital skills. She tells me that for people living in poverty, digital by default can leave them in an even more vulnerable position. 'The healthy start scheme is a great initiative that many families depend on, but since its application process has shifted online, digitally excluded families can't access these vouchers to buy essential healthy food items,' she tells me.

During the cost-of-living crisis in 2023, when inflation in the UK was at a forty-year high, the growing digital divide made accessing vital government support impossible for many. 'We have seen [digitally excluded] people unable to access the grants available to them, whether that's for bills, rent, universal credit or other types of support.' After requesting information using a Freedom of Information request in 2023, Age UK found that almost a third of London councils don't offer a way to apply for housing benefit or council tax rebates without having internet access.[13] The failure to tackle this is meaning a huge number of people are being disenfranchised due to the shift to digital modes of service provision, which is making the benefits of digital transformation inaccessible for those without digital skills.

This worrying pattern is unfolding nationwide. In 2023, the UK railway's industry body, the Rail Delivery Group, announced proposals to close nearly all of the UK's ticket offices, after the Transport Secretary Mark Harper wrote to the operator demanding they cut costs. Supposedly a plan to 'modernise customer service', the proposal was met with a huge backlash from customers across the UK, with the campaign to keep our ticket offices receiving the largest ever consultation response from the general public, with over 680,000 people expressing the vital need for our ticket offices. Disability charities condemned the decision for the impact that removing workers and replacing them with machines would have on disabled people. With 23 per cent of disabled adults having no access to the internet[14] and the Royal National Institute of Blind People estimating that only 3 per cent blind and partially sighted customers are able to use a machine,[15] this decision has struck campaigners as outright discriminatory.

Look to our schools, doctors' surgeries, post offices and supermarkets, and you'll see that more faces are being replaced with screens, where job losses are treated as collateral damage and our experience as customers becomes isolated and depersonalised. These examples are evidence of a system that prioritises digitisation for profit, rather than improving services for both workers and users. For corporations, apps and machines don't need training; they don't need to be paid a wage or a pension; there is a one-off installation cost; and the task is outsourced to the user. But at what human cost?

For railway workers, many of whom worked throughout the pandemic with minimal protections and support, it's estimated that ticket office closures would result in at least 2,000 job losses.[16] For customers, rather than ensuring that public transport is inclusive for all, the digital shift is only locking out those who are unable to navigate and use digital technology. As journalist Taj Ali writes, 'While it is true that most passengers now rely on ticket machines and online purchases, the depiction of station ticket offices as a relic of a bygone era is misleading and ignores the devastating impact their removal will have on passengers who rely on them.'[17] This is the type of ignorance in corporate and government decision-making that is leading to a widening digital divide. In the digital age, corporate greed and digital exclusion go hand in hand, with both customers and workers losing out as a result.

The inhumanity of the failure to provide non-digital options for services can be understood by speaking to anyone who has ever tried to access a digital service, only to be met with barriers, answering machines and auto-replies. In 2022, author Pete Paphides (@petepaphides) came to Twitter to share his late father's struggle to operate an online app to pay for parking at his friend's memorial service.[18] Lacking the digital skills to navigate this app, he called his son for help and asked him to find a number to speak to someone. But the company's operations were fully automated, with no humans to speak to for help. After his father died, a debt recovery service was deployed to chase the £100 fine debt. Not only was he digitally excluded from an essential task, but he was also penalised after his death as a result.

Our collective understanding of digital skills needs to change, shifting from viewing digital capabilities as an individual responsibility that we just have, to a collective duty where we support and learn from each other. Having digital skills benefits us all, they allow us to participate in society equally, and can improve our financial, social and mental wellbeing. Take a look around when you're out in public, and you can slowly notice the gaps that the switch to digital is already leaving in place, and the people losing out. Digital transformation cannot be something that is done *to us*, but is something that we must co-create at every stage.

In 2022, Spanish 78-year-old Carlos San Juan led a two-month-long campaign with the phrase 'I'm old, not stupid' to force governments and banks to offer dedicated services with humans, not machines, for those who can't use online banking.[19] Resistance to the outright replacement of in-person services, and dedication to ensuring that digital transformation is an inclusive process for all, will be led by us, not by tech companies who solely seek to cash in. We all deserve the right to choose whether we want to engage with services digitally or in person, and customers and workers must rally together to ensure that corporations don't just make these decisions for us. If we want offline options to remain in place, we need to show they're needed, we need to use them and demand that they are vital. The public consultation on closing UK railway ticket offices in 2023 witnessed over half a million people rally against it. This was a historic moment in our digital transition, which resulted in a government U-turn, a recognition that this was a short-sighted change that would exclude a vast number of people from an essential service.

Meeting Tony was a light-bulb moment for me. Being a Gen Z who has grown up online, what some may call a digital native, until I met Tony I was completely and blissfully ignorant of the bleak realities of digital exclusion and the impact this can have on your daily life. I had been unaware of the barriers to accessing and keeping up with a world that is shifting online faster each day, and the complex challenges that brings. When I met Tony, I was confronted by my own unconscious assumption that navigating smartphones and laptops, Wi-Fi and passwords, is as self-explanatory as it has been for me. But this is far from a reality for the vast majority of people. Since meeting Tony, we've developed an unlikely yet rewarding friendship. While I taught him practical skills like how to phone someone or download an app, Tony has taught me to pay more attention. He taught me to look around beyond my experience of the digital world; he taught me to look up from my phone and connect with people the old-fashioned way.

For everyone to benefit from digital transformation, digital skills must be understood as a fundamental aspect of universal education that everyone in the modern world has the right to. Some countries are already doing this. Mexico recognised internet provision as a constitutional right in 2013, Finland made internet access a legal right in 2010, and in 2021 the UN's Human Rights Council adopted a resolution on human rights on the internet, which called for all states to work towards closing the digital divide. These are all steps in the right direction. For too long, the widening digital divide has fallen on hard-working charities or helping hands to fix – be that a kind neighbour, a caring grandchild or a patient social worker. But digital access is a universal right that governments need to prioritise and enshrine in legislation. Only by understanding digital participation and access as a fundamental right can we ensure that our digital world is one that eradicates inequalities, rather than reproducing them.

CONCLUSION
Ctrl + Alt + Reclaim

'Fixing tech isn't more important than fixing everything else, but unless we fix tech, we can forget about winning any of those other fights.'

Cory Doctorow, *The Internet Con*[1]

We are at a precipice. The digital world is the thread which now binds us all. Whether you like it or not, digital technology is creeping its way into every area of our lives. But the benefits aren't being felt equally. More and more of us are waking up to the fact that Big Tech corporations have too much power and too much dominance over our everyday lives. The harms and human cost of the rise of technology cannot go ignored. I realised this in the hardest way possible when my sister passed, forced to reconcile the grim reality of the digital world that many see as being unimpeachable, unproblematic and entirely neutral. Tech was designed by humans and therefore it has the capacity to not only replicate our messes, biases and dangers, but worsen them and further their reach too.

This book could never contain all of the harms at play in the digital sphere, but I hope I have a captured a small amount of humanity to make you look at the devices and platforms you inhabit with a more critical eye. Now, I don't want to end the book without providing any solutions, any glimmer of hope for a future where we can have the agency to prevent harms from happening, where we can hold those in power to account to protect our loved ones. Therefore, this is a conclusion, but it is not the end, and I want to document as many options for you as possible so that this can be a catalyst for change for the better. There are many people already doing brilliant things and who have altered how technology works to be more ethical and considered, and I will highlight them here. But you are just as important in this.

Whether you are tired of impulsively scrolling, tired of spending the majority of your waking life staring at screens, tired of the false urgency and validation you've been conditioned to seek, tired of not knowing where your information is going and how our data is being used, or you are concerned for those you love, whether young, old or vulnerable, there are things to be done. Many are choosing to log off – a small act, but one that has significant impacts for our wellbeing and autonomy. On top of this, you have the power to hold others to account, because it should not be left up to us, the users, to protect ourselves.

Since digital technology is not only used by us, but about us and for us, in our healthcare services, our education institutions, by our governments, our police, our employers, it has to work for us intentionally. Ultimately, the online world is not going anywhere. The online world itself is where so many of us get most of our knowledge, opinions and news. Each day, digital devices become more entrenched into our daily activities, making them essential, not optional, and so it would be ignorant and unrealistic to suggest the way out is to quit using tech altogether, but we desperately need a remodelling of our digital world. It would be wrong to fear technology, but for all the issues this book has explored, I understand it's easy to. That's why we vitally need a movement that centres the reclamation of technology in our collective interests, rather than a rejection of it entirely.

Most of this book has explored the experiences of those who have lost out to digital technology, who have experienced it as a force for harm rather than good. It has explored the hidden stories of those who have fallen victim to techno-solutionism, in a world that ignores the risks and realities of a digital world that puts profit first, and our lives second. Capitalist expansion at speed always results in a human cost, and we see this consistently throughout history. During colonialism, the rapid industrialisation of Britain came at the cost of those in the colonies, their lives and their economies taking the hit whilst the UK benefited from this process of extraction and expansion. Progress has too often been a buzzword that evades all accountability and consideration of what it means and for whom. This is the same dilemma, one that has simply taken a new form. Will we put people over profit? Will our digital world be one that empowers all, or just empowers an already powerful minority? Will we seize the innovative tools to remake our world for the better, or will they simply serve the same old interests of those in power? So what is to be done? Here are my seven suggestions of solutions that could help us build a more humane digital future.

New rules for a new world

For far too long, Big Tech companies have been treated with a culture of impunity that has not only enabled but empowered them to wreak havoc on our mental wellbeing, our democracies, our autonomy, our relationships, our work lives. Scandals like the Cambridge Analytica scandal and the Pegasus Spyware scandal have quickly become old news while tech companies are given a slap on the wrist and asked to behave better. The UK government has taken a 'pro-innovation' stance on regulation, a euphemism for slow and reluctant, because regulating means putting the interests and safeguards of people over profit. Like when the tobacco industry was regulated, and cigarette adverts on television were banned because it became clear that this was having severe impacts on our health and wellbeing, we must hold the tech industry to account in the same way.

Self-regulation does not work on its own. Social media can be addictive and creates a dependency not dissimilar to drugs and alcohol, so it's only right we look at enacting similar restrictions to protect public health.

Campaigners, policy makers and NGOs have already begun doing the work of demanding greater regulation. The EU's AI Act, Digital Services Act and the UK's Online Safety Act have emerged in the past five years and aim to hold tech companies to account and keep users safe. However, they don't go far enough, and we urgently need to update existing legislation to include the digital sphere. The Suicide Act, for example, was introduced before the internet existed, and therefore although assisted suicide is a crime, in a digital capacity it can go unpunished and unrecognised. There are loopholes in the legislation where harm can be done, so it's vital we supplement existing laws while also working on new ones.

Creating specific laws is vital, but we also need an overarching framework that recognises that in our digital world, our human and digital rights are not inseparable. A Universal Declaration of Digital Rights could be the mechanism by which Big Tech platforms and governments are held to account and we, the people, uphold our digital rights. This wouldn't be a silver bullet, but in times of harm it would give us a tool to hold those in power to account, the same way that the Universal Declaration of Human Rights is used to enshrine and uphold our rights when these are violated or are at risk of being infringed upon.

Since our digital and offline lives are so intertwined, it's only right that the rights and protections we have offline are mirrored and implemented online. As well as this, our digital world now requires a different form of governance, especially given the increasing proximity between tech leaders and political leaders, tech corporations and governments. Author James Muldoon has proposed the creation of a Global Digital Services Organisation to place a levy on Big Tech and to make the digital economy more democratic. Events like the UK's AI Safety Summit could be an opportunity for progressive change, but only if we – the stakeholders, the users – occupy space in the decision-making conversations.

Undeniably, Big Tech has come to be one of the most powerful industries in the world, so we have to put our money where our mouth is. Incentivising social media companies to make their platforms safe looks like punishing them financially when they are not. Money is the language these companies understand and respond to, so it is one of the most efficient ways to demand behavioural change. The Molly Rose Foundation proposes that the same way the 'polluter pays' principle applies to holding fossil fuel companies to account for their climate harms, this should be reflected for Big Tech corporations, and introducing a one-off harm reduction windfall tax would force tech companies to effectively make their platforms safer for children and young people. Fines are another measure already being used to hold tech companies to account, with Apple and Google being fined for monopolistic and greedy behaviour such as breaking competition laws and intellectual property rules, but occasional fines alone are not enough. These companies also need to be contributing financially to the countries they operate in and profit from, since without our unpaid labour and data they would cease to exist. Tech companies must pay the corporation tax they owe if we are to benefit equally from their 'innovation' too. By regulating Big Tech we keep them accountable and under control, and by restricting them we prevent growing harms in the digital sphere and beyond.

Safety by design

If tech companies adopted a safety by design approach, we wouldn't have to resort to digital detoxes to look after our mental health. The reason that social media is currently so bad for us is because it has not been designed with our wellbeing in mind. If tech was designed with users' needs and wants from the get-go, algorithms would make this distinction between harmful and helpful content, rather than sending us spiralling down whatever rabbit hole lures us in. Instead of being addictive and predatory, and preying on our vulnerabilities, exposing us to content that puts us at risk of mental and even physical harm, algorithms could easily be designed to keep us safe online. This approach could save lives. Stories like my sister's, Archie Battersbee's and Molly Russell's are evidence of what is at stake when safety is not at the forefront of digital design.

Safety and wellbeing start at the root, in the design process. People vs Big Tech is calling for the engagement-based algorithms and recommender systems to be turned off. These systems are consistently detrimental and fuel radicalisation, despair, addiction, polarisation and division. Only by disrupting this process will we be safe from harm, including harm to democracy, harm to our loved ones, harm to our mental health and harm to our planet. It is *not* the user's responsibility to keep ourselves safe when we choose to use these platforms, and our lives can no longer be treated as collateral damage for dysfunctional design. Tech innovators, designers and builders must centre safety as a pillar of the design process. As journalist Kashmir Hill writes: 'The countless decisions a creator makes about the architecture of a technology's platform shape the way that users will interact with it.' The industry's designers, engineers, founders and builders hold immense power in our digital world, power that will determine our future. The World Economic Forum recommends that 'rather than retrofitting safeguards after an issue has occurred, Safety by Design [. . .] can minimise online threats by anticipating, detecting and eliminating online harms before they occur.' Many digital rights organisations are rallying for Big Tech companies to centre ethical and humane design principles, such as Design It For Us in America and 5Rights in the UK.

A brilliant example of Safety by Design in practice is R;pple, the search engine tool that intercepts harmful searches and signposts vulnerable people to support services. The team also tests its technology for abusability by conducting threat modelling at multiple stages of the design life cycle. These are trauma-informed design principles that can lead to more human-centred technology. Our technology should be aspirational ethically, and truly represent a society we want to live in. This is why we must have a voice in shaping, building and creating tech, through surveys and active integration into decisions made by the Big Tech players. Safety is really just the beginning and it's the bare minimum. I want a digital world that isn't just safe but actually empowering and liberating. A digital ecosystem where diversity and connection can thrive, where our differences draw us together instead of tearing us apart.

Tech can no longer be gatekept

This leads me to my next point. While writing this book, I consistently found myself in awe of the knowledge and practical solutions that many of those who had experienced harms could offer. There are so many people who are armed with the insight and understanding to fix the problems we face, but if the gatekeepers won't listen, then we are stuck. When we lost Aimee, I quickly became disappointed and tired of hearing decision-makers say that they just didn't know what to do, and tech executives claiming they were trying their best. I was exhausted from the toll of having to recount our loss over and over to strangers, in the hope that they might pay attention to trigger change. For us who had lost a loved one, the solutions were glaringly obvious: we need regulation and policies that safeguard vulnerable people and an algorithm that directs people away from harmful content and towards support. These two things might have helped Aimee.

Similarly, the women's rights campaigners I spoke to about technology-facilitated abuse consistently expressed to me the vital need for those in the tech industry to recognise potential ill uses of their products, and to introduce measures that would prevent them. If you have people who have experienced digital harms involved in the design process then you have people who will recognise what safety measures would prevent others having similar experiences in the future. Our lived experiences of online harms had made us experts in online safety almost overnight. So if you are a policy maker, a Big Tech employee or a politician reading this, I urge you to do something beyond just listening. I urge you to invite those who are directly impacted into the spaces where ideas become reality, and action the solutions that they suggest. I can promise they will not only make your job easier but they will suggest things you never would have come up with. When our technology is no longer an aside to our lives, but is becoming the fabric of the social system we live in, we must all have a say in the decisions around these tools which will determine our future.

Verity Harding is an expert in AI and policymaking who coined the phrase 'democratic deficit' to describe the knowledge gap between those in the tech industry making decisions and those in government making policy. There has always been a divide between STEM fields and the humanities, but in our digital world, we can no longer siphon ourselves off in this way. Greater collaboration between all fields in relation to technological transformation is vital if we are to create a humane digital future. So far, unions across the globe have been pioneering the fight against exploitative technologies and leading a resistance that recognises how important it is that we reclaim the digital world from the ground up. The Trades Union Congress recently drafted the Artificial Intelligence Bill, which if passed would be the first law relating to the use of AI at work in the UK. It would enshrine in law concrete obligations and rights that would protect workers from inhumane algorithmic management and surveillance and empower them to challenge automated decision-making processes.

Sneha Revanur is a brilliant example of someone who is breaking the barriers to decision-making that for so long have been gatekept by the Big Tech elite. With her work as president of Encode Justice, the organisation she founded at fifteen, she is a strong advocate of holding representatives to account, and she became the youngest civil society leader invited to an AI roundtable with Vice President Kamala Harris. By combining youth organising across university campuses globally alongside meeting with representatives and lawmakers, her work is influencing policy decisions that are shaping our digital future.

She also recognises the unique position that young people occupy in the digital world, and the innate knowledge that comes with growing up online. 'People might not realise it but we're actually interacting with AI and digital technology all around us and I think young people are aware of that and have always been aware that there is this digital apparatus hanging over us and that is influencing decisions that impact our lives.' As a young person who has grown up online, I recognise the potential of my generation to transform our digital future for the better as limitless. I believe young people have a pivotal role to play in co-creating our digital world, because the digital future is our future.

A digital curriculum

I was part of the last generation of children that grew up without smartphones and tablets, but part of the first generation of teenagers who had social media. I know what it was like before and after. I've seen the hopeful ambitions of tech founders become distant memories compared to where we are now. Our young people are experiencing a crisis of confidence, which is fuelling mental health issues, self-harm and risky behaviour online and offline. Many of the young lives that have been lost to suicide in recent years have come after these children have themselves fallen victim to predators or abusers online, and don't know whom to turn to as a result. Meanwhile, parents and teachers understandably don't feel equipped to tackle the sheer scale of what is happening, meaning that children are left to figure it out for themselves. But we cannot afford to be passive, because to leave young people to figure out the digital world for themselves is to leave them vulnerable and exposed.

As a lived experience campaigner who grew up in the digital age, I've met with politicians and government officials to advocate for our young people and I've heard from teachers, parents and youth campaigners. What has become clear from these discussions is the urgent need for digital education that teaches children and young people how to stay safe online, and makes it clear to them that they are not alone or to blame if something bad happens to them online. Teaching children that it is not their fault if they experience an online harm could prevent them from spiralling into despair and instead encourage them to speak openly with their parents or teachers about what they've gone through. This would empower young people to lead safer and healthier digital lives and it would ensure that teachers and parents are equipped to have conversations with their young people about any incidents that happen online. Young people should not just be taught the benefits of digital technology or the practical uses of these tools, but how to protect themselves, how to report abuse or harmful content and how to log off if they feel they need to.

Beyond this, we must teach children about how social media algorithms work. Teenagers need to understand that the current design of social media platforms makes us feel emotions on an extreme scale, and education should facilitate them with mindfulness techniques and strategies to develop emotional resilience. If teenagers were taught how algorithms target them with content they predict they will engage with, this could help them to approach these platforms with critical thinking. It could mean that boys are more likely to call out and report sexist behaviour online. It could mean that girls are able to see content that promotes eating disorders and recognise that this is unhealthy and toxic. Parents Hollie Battersbee and Lisa Kenevan, who have both lost children to dangerous online challenges, launched a campaign called Be Challenge Aware, to teach children how to be cautious of risky online trends. Healthy challenges and differences in opinion are essential, and we need to help teenagers understand the same is true online, but what is unacceptable is trolling and abuse. They need to understand the real-life implications digital harms can have, just like schools do with driving, drugs and smoking. All of these interventions would make young people feel more agency in their own digital lives and would make them equipped to lead digital lives that are healthy and happy.

Yet it isn't only children and young people who need a digital curriculum. Training and investment into digital skills at every level, not just in school, but in apprenticeships, workplaces, community hubs and adult courses is essential in ensuring that no one is left behind. Andrew Pakes is the deputy general secretary at Prospect, a trade union that represents over 150,000 members in the UK. He believes that what is needed is a digital transition. Like the Green New Deal is a plan to create economies that are good for people and the planet by investing in job creation and renewable energy sources, a digital transition would help communities, workers and the economy successfully manage the introduction of new technologies into our world. 'The wide impact of digital technologies on communities and workspaces requires a coordinated approach on skills and industrial strategy to address issues around job opportunities, digital inclusion and regional inequalities. Skills need to be central to this mission.' Rapid technological transformation can reap immense societal rewards, but only if we prioritise inclusive integration and implementation; upskilling the population alongside the introduction of new tools is a core part of an equitable digital future.

A cultural shift

It's time that we collectively start challenging Big Tech's ego problem, and what the industry's ruthless desire for profit means for our lives, and ask ourselves is this really what we want? It's becoming clearer each day that digital technology will not fix all our problems and is often fuelling them instead. From the wrongful firings of workers, to creating art devoid of human passion and emotion, to censoring our fights for freedom and liberation, it's evident that machines and computers are no replacement for humans. Technology can no longer be framed as the solution to our collective problems, when it is creating, and reinventing, so many of them.

Since ChatGPT came to prominence in 2022, technologists such as Joy Buolamwini, Meredith Whittaker, Timnit Gebru and Safiya Noble have spoken out to express that we ought to stop fearing an AI doomsday and instead focus on the problems in the here and now. Technology can be a distraction, beyond being a harmful form of progress, and we cannot afford to lose sight of what's important in the world. Technological developments should not be at odds with humanity and our collective wellbeing, and we cannot afford for people's lives to become collateral damage. My mum once told me that from her experience of growing up in a rural village, you either grow up never wanting to leave or you cannot wait for the day to escape. I think our current relationship with technology is like that. We sit at opposite ends of the spectrum, our opinions polarised. You have those who avoid using it at all costs, and those who are totally immersed in its grasp. Instead, we need a balanced view, and a cultural shift towards healthy criticism and technology as an active tool, not a passive distraction.

This will take time. For centuries, science and technology have been heralded as superior to other types of knowledge. This is why we equate technology to objectivity, to truth. But we must understand that technology is human by its very nature of being created by us, so it is more of a mirror than a future. Techno-solutionism only benefits those who profit from the technification of every aspect of our lives. As writer P.E. Moskowitz said: 'We don't need parks, libraries, beautiful architecture and public transit if we can be convinced to conduct our lives in a virtual fashion. This saves governments from needing to invest in the real-world . . . it acts as an enabler of austerity politics.'[2]

At the heart of so much tech optimism in our times and throughout history is the argument that tech will make our lives more efficient and productive. But is this what we need in these times? When increased efficiency has a negative impact on our health, our relationships and our collective wellbeing, perhaps the sacrifice is too great. Perhaps convenience is not good for us. I believe we should aim for what IEET (Institute for Ethics and Emerging Technologies) calls 'technoprogressive' orientation, which is a framework for how tech can be used for our collective goals and happiness. Digital technology needs to be something we can choose to embrace and immerse ourselves in or let go of completely at our leisure. Agency is fundamental to our digital future. We ought to be able to have boundaries with our digital tools, the same way we might with a job, a relationship, a hobby or where we live. But right now digital is often the default. Slowing down and pausing to consider whether these technologies are beneficial, productive or empowering before we adopt them, is the opposite of what tech leaders want, but it's what we collectively need. Slowing down is fundamental to a degrowth agenda, which recognises the harms that endless consumption is having. Discernment is key for us to self-regulate, but the cultural shift needs to extend out to those in power and in control. This cultural shift will help to make regulation and safety by design happen, because it will prevent Big Tech from having unending access to every part of our lives and minds.

Redefining connection

When social media launched, many of us ran into its warm embrace. The early years of the internet glistened with possibility, and brought us far-reaching connection on a level we had never previously been able to experience. The creators of these tools touted their abilities to take our social and personal lives to new heights, deepening existing connections and creating new ones. But today, those same tools have had the opposite effect, and many of us feel alienated, isolated and lonelier than ever. Social media has bred division, fuelled polarisation and amplified the individualism that breaks down community and connection.

Redefining connection is more a reclamation of the human values we all share than a creation of something new. We need to rediscover the desire for connection, for self-expression and discovery beyond digital barriers once again. The same motivations that drew us to social media in the first place show that these values exist within us at our core, by nature of being social animals. For many of us, sharing is the language through which we connect; it is the foundation on which we build our relationships. Sharing is the gateway to friendship, conversation and self-expression, but it is one that can only truly unfold if we do it offline. Connection in the digital age requires a switch. A switch between existing more online than we do offline.

We must ask ourselves: how can we truly experience the embodiment of social connection within the limitations of a screen? The reality is, you can't. It is a mere illusion of it, but that's all. So, how can we meet new people with different or similar interests to us within the communities that we already have? How can we centre connection and self-expression in our lives without reaching for our phones? These are questions that may feel hard to answer initially, but it is our digital immersion that has made these things feel difficult. The reality is very simple. Redefining connection could look like befriending your neighbours, or sparking up a conversation with an old friend. It might come in the form of joining a new club in your community, or volunteering your time with a cause you're passionate about. Since spending more time offline while writing this book, I've taken up aerial yoga and hiking. I've got back into reading fiction and started a book club with my friend. I've made time for new friendships that don't purely exist online, with people of all ages and backgrounds. These are the things that are possible when we make more time for our lives offline, and realise that the illusion of connection we are drawn to on our feeds can actually exist in our material lives, with many more benefits too.

When I'm feeling at my lowest, all I want is a hug or a hand to hold. I'll call my mum to hear her reassurance about whatever is causing me stress. I'm drawn to my partner's arms as a comfort blanket when the stress of daily life feels all-consuming, and I feel immediately soothed. Most of the time, we just need someone to lean on. Humans are excellent at alleviating stress in each other, often without even intending to. Eye contact alone increases the feel-good hormone oxytocin, which reduces our cortisol levels almost immediately. Connection is something innately human, and it is deeply important for our wellbeing. It's no wonder that most mental health campaigns today emphasise the importance of talking to someone.

But today, connection has taken on a whole new meaning. In the digital age, human touch cannot and should not be replaced by a digital alternative. Simply, some of us still prefer a friendly face over a screen. In the Netherlands, supermarkets are pushing back against the shift to self-service checkouts. One supermarket chain has created 'chat checkouts' where customers can go to take extra time to have a chat whilst they do their shop. Especially in contexts where we need to talk to someone about sensitive and complex issues like our health, or financial support, a screen with a voice won't cut it. Many of us, including me, already struggle to get answering machines to direct our calls to the right person, so how can we expect entire services to be automated and give us what we need? We all deserve the freedom to choose whether we go digital, and anyone who provides a service has the responsibility to make this choice available to all. Whilst artificial intelligence and chatbots might be able to complete the same tasks more rapidly, they will never be able to offer the value that human connection brings us time and time again.

Get involved

So why don't we all just log off? We should not have to remove ourselves from the digital world in order to be content, and it's simply unrealistic in today's digital age. This isn't to say we shouldn't take steps to spend less time online – I'm a huge advocate for limiting screen time and regulating our content diet as an act of self-care and preservation, and as I've just said, more time for human connection is immensely valuable. However, I am also someone who has experienced the benefits of connection, creativity, collaboration and relationship building that the online world can bring, and I don't believe it's fair to simply tell us to deal with it or log off entirely. As it stands, the digital world is being created and built by the few for the few, yet it's where so many of us spend the majority of our time. Instead, I believe we have the collective potential to radically change the digital world for the better into one that we are content with, and one that is beneficial to our wellbeing and joy. This is why our communities, who make up digital users, must be at the forefront of decision-making and co-creating our digital infrastructure. We have adapted to become both dependent and required to be online in some form, so we have to make the digital world work for us.

Getting involved can take so many forms. You may consider joining a campaign or movement advocating for our digital rights, such as Open Rights Group, Smartphone Free Childhood, Encode Justice or Not Your Porn. Collaborative campaigns such as these can witness profound wins when it comes to holding Big Tech and governments to account. Fight for the Future is a group of artists, engineers, activists and technologists who have organised some of the largest online protests in history, channelling internet outrage into political power. Political change is vital for protecting our rights in a digital world, so writing to your MPs on these issues is essential for holding them to account and ensuring that they represent our collective interests. You could also attend protests and demonstrations that target Big Tech and show we will not be complacent in their continued exploitation of people and planet.

Another method is boycotting. Too often, when it comes to our digital devices, users forget to recognise our power as consumers. Disrupting these monopolies and ditching platforms when they don't serve us is one way we can use our consumer power to influence how these companies behave. We can bring the same energy we bring to fast fashion and fossil fuel companies to these social media platforms, boycotting them and disallowing them from mining our emotional lives; the recent number of people and businesses leaving X is a good example of this. However, I do appreciate there are limitations to this as many people's livelihoods are linked to these platforms, yet even just a day of collective action could be enough to have a lasting impact.

Lastly, we need to get offline more. I have undergone a journey of gradually decentring the central role that digital technology plays in my life. I have detached myself more from notifications, content and online debates, disallowing them from having too much of an impact over my mood and my attention. This is a behavioural change that will not be easy, due to the habits we have entrenched into our everyday lives. But there are steps to take to lessen your digital intake such as simply leaving your phone downstairs overnight so it isn't the last thing you see before bed or the first thing you see in the morning, placing screen time restrictions on your phone and not using social media at the weekends or in the evenings.

Opt for human faces over automated options in your daily life to show businesses that we value real connection over technological 'convenience'. Take your nieces and nephews to explore the outdoors together instead of sitting inside in front of a shared screen. Arrange to meet that friend in person rather than spending an hour on FaceTime; you never know just how much better it feels to be sitting alongside someone you love until you remind yourself by doing it. Sign up to your local library to keep alive the third spaces that digital platforms are rapidly replacing. Our dependency is something we can unlearn, and taking a small step away each day can end up being a great leap over the course of a month, and vast progress over a year.

These are suggestions that you can take with you into the world. They are not the only way for you to be a part of change, but they should give you some sense of how you can improve your own digital future, and that of others too.

This book has been about the human costs of the digital world. I am not an expert in technology nor a leader in a Big Tech firm, but what I am is a human being who had an incredible sister, a sister who was lost to the harms of an industry that believes it is beyond reproach. I speak from my lived experience as someone directly impacted, and I used my skills as a journalist to give voice to others who have been impacted too. We all understand implicitly that the digital world is unsafe, and while I don't want you to be afraid after reading this book, I do hope you will have been shocked and that your eyes will have been opened. If we are not aware of the harmful digital realities, and those people who are reeling from their impact, how can we ever repair the digital landscape? This book is a step, I hope, to helping you to look more critically at the devices you use and the platforms you inhabit. It is a plea from someone who has experienced such horrific loss to see clearly that digital technology can never and will never be neutral.

The time to act is now. Big Tech has unleashed floodgates of harms, and we are struggling to keep our heads above water. We shouldn't wait for the tide to sweep us away before we build a dam to stop it. I hope this book has shown how we all have stakes in reclaiming the digital world from Big Tech. Whether we lose out to our free time because we're being conditioned to be addicted to scrolling, or we lose the option to chat with a human about our health or banking because public services have become digitised or we are abused through the digital devices that were supposed to aid us, or like me, we lose a loved one, the majority of us are facing digital harms, even if we are not completely cognisant of it yet.

The digital world may seem so expansive that it cannot be reined in or contained, but this is not true. We can always choose. We can embrace the peace that time offline can grant us while choosing when and how to spend our time online. We can choose to prioritise offline connection instead of fuelling online division. We can use digital tech, instead of us being used by Big Tech. We can choose the digital future we want, but it requires us to lend our voice to change. A humane digital future can sound like a juxtaposition since we have been led to view technology as non-human, but this is not true – it is an extension and invention of humanity. Tech was created by us, and so it can be remade by us too.

Acknowledgements

Thank you to my mum and dad for taking Aimee and me to the library almost every weekend and developing my love for reading and writing from a tender age. Thank you for always having a copy of the *Mirror* and the *Guardian* on the table at the weekends and sparking my fascination for reading and telling people's stories. Mum: thank you for being my number one fan. Your sheer determination has been my road map from a young age. Thank you for your prayers, your strength, and for making me breakfasts and lunches for a solid year so I didn't have to waste any time on my writing days. Dad: thanks for teaching me the importance of writing and speaking up by writing to the *Guardian* at any slight inconvenience or political annoyance. Thank you to my extended family who have supported us through our grief; we could not have got through it without you. Thank you to Umi, Jo, Vildan, Sirin, Karen and the countless strong women who have poured into my life from childhood, you all inspired me in so many ways.

Without the people whom I interviewed for this book sharing their experiences, *Logging Off* wouldn't exist. I

cannot express my gratitude enough for every person
who shared theirs for trusting me to tell your stories and
for opening up to me about some of the most painful
and intimate parts of your life. Tony – what can I say?
You taught me to look beyond my own bubble of digital
experiences and meeting you pushed me to connect the
dots, and without you this book wouldn't exist. A huge
thank you to Ian Russell for your relentless work to make
the digital world a safe place and for your resilience and
support, and to the Bereaved Families for Online Safety
group, a club that no one ever wants to be a part of, but
a club of inspiring individuals without whom I could not
keep doing this. I also want to give a special mention to
Andy Burrows at the Molly Rose Foundation and the
brilliant team at Leigh Day.

Thank you to my editor Katie Ogunsakin for taking a
chance on a debut author and giving me the opportunity
to tell my story. Thank you to my agent Megan Staunton
for taking me on, championing me and for your kind
support and empathy at every step of the way. Thank
you to Mireille Harper for being the first person to hear
of *Logging Off* when it was just an idea and for seeing the
vision. I am so grateful for you constantly sharing your
wisdom and knowledge, and for the constant reminders
of emotional support navigating this journey. Thank you
to the women authors who have shared their time, tips
and words of encouragement – you each helped me feel so
much less alone in this, including Grace, Emily, Shahed
and Mikaela; I appreciate you a lot.

Thank you to every person in the tech justice space who has taken the time to share their knowledge with me. I'm indebted to Tanya O'Carroll and Sanne Thijssen from People vs Big Tech for all of the opportunities you've shared, kindness you've shown me and for helping me feel less like an imposter in this space. Thank you to everyone at the People vs Big Tech bootcamp for listening with kindness and compassion, and for being a beautiful bunch of people to fight with. I never thought I'd write a book about technology, and I've been privileged to learn from some amazing people who have helped me along the way; a special thanks to Mary Towers at the TUC, Jeni and Adam at Connected by Data, Elena Michael at Not Your Porn. Claire Farrell for being an inspiration. Charlie at Hard Art for the affirmations. Seyi at Glitch, for the reminder to take care of myself and my body. Thank you to all of the people who have been campaigning, fighting and calling for a digital world that empowers us all – I hope this book shines a light on the path you are already paving and brings more comrades along the way.

Thank you, Jesse, for supporting me through the hardest period of my life, for easing my endless anxieties about my first book, for being my escape and for the unconditional love you show me. Thank you to the beautiful and selfless women who I am lucky to call my friends: Romalie, India, Shante, Steph, Erin, Sheila, Trinn, Makena, Esme – our commune is my safe haven. Yasmin, for always reminding me to give myself grace and for your prayers and affirmations. Erin, for always listening, and for being my ranting partner. Romalie, my non-spirit guide, for the beautiful poem and handwritten cards, for being an absolute rock of emotional support these past few years. I love you all so much.

Thank you to the team at NEON – I would not be able to cope speaking on radio and TV without your incredible training! Thank you to the Society of Authors and Journalists Charity for their financial support, which allowed me to spend time writing this book outside of paid work. Thank you to all of the editors who have commissioned me to write – you've each helped me get here.

Thank you to the teachers who poured their time and affirmations into me and for pushing me to challenge myself from a young age. I especially want to thank my psychology A level teacher Kieran for pushing me to pursue my own path. That conversation in your classroom changed my life forever.

I want to mention that without the incredible writers and authors who have inspired me with their own words, I would have never shared my own. Reading other brilliant writers' work was how I learned to write, so thank you to those who have come before me, for giving me the channel that I cannot imagine life without.

Thank you to each person who has ever read my words, especially those who remember A Note of Despair – this book wouldn't exist without you.

Endnotes

Introduction: Welcome to the New World

1   https://www.nobelprize.org/prizes/peace/1964/king/lecture/
2   https://www.theguardian.com/media/2024/feb/12/brianna-ghey-mother-warns-tech-bosses-more-children-will-die-without-action

Chapter 1: The Double Life of a Digital Native

1   https://x.com/Noahpinion/status/902301308702515202
2   Twenge, J. M., Joiner, T. E., Rogers, M. L., & Martin, G. N. (2018). 'Increases in Depressive Symptoms, Suicide-Related Outcomes, and Suicide Rates Among U.S. Adolescents After 2010 and Links to Increased New Media Screen Time'. *Clinical Psychological Science*, 6(1), 2018, 3-17. https://doi.org/10.1177/2167702617723376
3   https://www.nytimes.com/interactive/2021/12/09/us/where-the-despairing-log-on.html
4   Ibid.
5   https://www.ic3.gov/Media/Y2023/PSA230912
6   https://www.mdpi.com/2227-9067/9/12/1889
7   https://www.thesun.co.uk/news/17535301/son-killed-himself-online-suicide-forum-shut-down-now/
8   https://www.npr.org/2022/10/09/1127686507/amazon-suicide-teenagers-poison

9   https://news.bloomberglaw.com/us-law-week/suicides-spur-suits-on-amazon-sales-of-legal-but-lethal-compound

10 https://www.independent.co.uk/news/uk/home-news/screen-time-damaging-psychologist-study-six-hours-average-a8237441.html

11 https://www.cagoldberglaw.com/cagoldberg-pllc-amazon-sodium-nitrite-lawsuit/

12 http://eprints.lse.ac.uk/67881/1/Gorzig_Adolescents%E2%80%99%20viewing_2016.pdf

13 https://www.ncbi.nlm.nih.gov/pmc/articles/PMC8910292/

14 https://www.gov.uk/government/publications/online-safety-act-explainer/online-safety-act-explainer

Chapter 2: Mining Your Business

1   https://www.economist.com/open-future/2019/01/21/we-need-to-own-our-data-as-a-human-right-and-be-compensated-for-it

2   https://www.globalactionplan.org.uk/our-work/online-climate/end-surveillance-advertising-to-kids

3   Mejias, Ulises A. and Couldry, Nick, *Data Grab* (WH Allen, 2024), pp. 3–6.

4   *The Great Hack* (Netflix, 2019).

5   https://www.theguardian.com/technology/2018/jul/26/facebook-market-cap-falls-109bn-dollars-after-growth-shock

6   https://www.theguardian.com/business/2023/oct/16/uk-lost-out-on-2bn-in-tax-in-2021-as-big-tech-shifted-profits-abroad-claim-campaigners

7   https://markets.businessinsider.com/news/stocks/apple-stock-market-cap-3-trillion-world-gdp-economies-france-2023-12

8   'Democracy at Risk in Davos: new report exposes big tech lobbying and political interference', Balanced Economy Project, 15 January 2025.

Chapter 3: The Algorithm in the Room

1   https://www.tiktok.com/@lukeandpete/
    video/7248936952215522586
2   https://dictionary.cambridge.org/dictionary/english/algorithm
3   https://www.kcl.ac.uk/news/masculinity-and-womens-equality
    -study-finds-emerging-gender-divide-in-young-peoples-attitudes
4   Siva Vaidhyanathan, *Antisocial Media* (Oxford University Press,
    2018), p.132.
5   https://counterhate.com/wp-content/uploads/2022/12/CCDH-
    Deadly-by-Design_120922.pdf
6   Amnesty International, 'Driven into Darkness: How TikTok's
    "For You" Feed Encourages Self-Harm and Suicidal Ideation, p.6.
    https://www.amnesty.org/en/documents/pol40/7350/2023/en/
7   https://news.sky.com/story/health-and-wellbeing-biggest-con-
    cern-for-young-people-survey-finds-13101695
8   https://www.theguardian.com/us-news/2024/feb/15/new-york-
    city-sues-social-media-addiction-kids-tiktok-instagram
9   https://www.redcross.org.uk/stories/disasters-and-emergencies/
    world/whats-happening-in-gaza-humanitarian-crisis-grows
10 https://www.hrw.org/report/2023/12/21/metas-broken-promises/
    systemic-censorship-palestine-content-instagram-and
11 https://www.propublica.org/article/facebook-hate-speech-cen-
    sorship-internal-documents-algorithms
12 https://www.newarab.com/news/malaysian-roblox-game-pro-
    palestine-protest-goes-viral
13 https://www.instagram.com/p/Cy5dxlzsiJO/?igshid=MzRlODBiN-
    WFlZA%3D%3D&img_index=1
14 https://www.media.mit.edu/projects/gender-shades/overview/
15 https://www.bbc.co.uk/news/technology-33347866
16 https://www.theguardian.com/technology/2015/may/20/google-
    apologises-racist-google-maps-white-house-search-results
17 https://unesdoc.unesco.org/ark:/48223/pf0000367416

18 https://www.foxglove.org.uk/2020/08/17/we-put-a-stop-to-the-a-level-grading-algorithm/

19 https://bigbrotherwatch.org.uk/2023/05/understanding-live-facial-recognition-statistics/

20 https://www.theguardian.com/newsletters/2023/aug/15/techscape-facial-recognition-software-detroit-porcha-woodruff-black-people-ai

21 https://www.theguardian.com/commentisfree/2023/may/08/ai-machines-hallucinating-naomi-klein

22 https://www.independent.co.uk/news/uk/home-news/facial-recognition-london-inaccurate-met-police-trials-a8898946.html

Chapter 4: Social Media as the Slot Machine

1 https://www.theguardian.com/technology/2017/dec/11/facebook-former-executive-ripping-society-apart

2 Bhargava VR, Velasquez M. 'Ethics of the Attention Economy: The Problem of Social Media Addiction'. *Business Ethics Quarterly.* 2021;31(3):321-359. doi:10.1017/beq.2020.32

3 https://www.simplypsychology.org/operant-conditioning.html

4 Hadar, A. A., Hadas, I., Lazarovits, A., Alyagon, U., Eliraz, D., and Zangen, A. (2017). 'Answering the missed call: Initial exploration of cognitive and electrophysiological changes associated with smartphone use and abuse'. *PLOS ONE,* 12(7), e0180094. https://doi.org/10.1371/journal.pone.0180094

5 https://www.theguardian.com/science/2022/jan/02/attention-span-focus-screens-apps-smartphones-social-media

6 https://www.purewow.com/wellness/tiktok-brain-explained

7 https://guilfordjournals.com/doi/epdf/10.1521/jscp.2018.37.10.751

8 https://www.priorygroup.com/media-centre/more-than-two-thirds-of-parents-think-government-should-introduce-digital-age-of-consent.

9 Cal Newport, *Digital Minimalism* (Portfolio, 2019), p.168

Chapter 5: Can Anyone Be Safe Online?

1 https://www.theguardian.com/technology/2018/jan/19/tim-cook-i-dont-want-my-nephew-on-a-social-network

2 https://metro.co.uk/2022/10/26/judge-rules-tiktok-cannot-be-held-responsible-for-10-year-olds-death-17645556/

3 https://www.womenshealthmag.com/health/a38603617/black-out-challenge-tiktok-2021/

4 https://www.independent.co.uk/news/world/americas/tik-tok-blackout-challenge-nylah-anderson-lawsuit-b2603370.html

5 https://news.bloomberglaw.com/us-law-week/section-230-should-not-be-big-techs-get-out-of-court-free-card

6 https://www.theverge.com/2022/7/7/23199058/tiktok-law-suits-blackout-challenge-children-death

7 https://www.statista.com/topics/12237/media-usage-in-the-unit-ed-kingdom/#topicOverview

8 https://www.amnesty.org/en/documents/pol40/7350/2023/en/

9 https://www.bridgealliance.us/addressing_negativity_bias_impact_on_social_media

10 https://www.amnesty.org/en/latest/news/2023/11/tik-tok-risks-pushing-children-towards-harmful-content/

11 https://www.psypost.org/from-likes-to-anxiety-examin-ing-the-psychological-costs-of-social-media-among-teens/

12 https://www.ofcom.org.uk/__data/assets/pdf_file/0026/280655/Understanding-Pathways-to-Online-Violent-Con-tent-Among-Children.pdf

13 https://www.theguardian.com/technology/2022/sep/30/how-molly-russell-fell-into-a-vortex-of-despair-on-social-media

14 https://arstechnica.com/tech-policy/2022/09/coroner-lists-insta-gram-algorithm-as-contributing-cause-of-uk-teens-death/

15 https://www.theguardian.com/technology/2022/oct/09/delays-online-safety-bill-endanger-young-people-molly-russell-father

16 https://www.bloomberg.com/news/features/2023-04-20/tiktok-effects-on-mental-health-in-focus-after-teen-suicide

17 https://www.theguardian.com/technology/2024/mar/16/
instagram-meta-lotte-rubaek-adviser-quits-failure-to-remove-
self-harm-content-

Chapter 6: What's Angry, Divisive and Spreads Fake News?

1 https://tobiasrose.medium.com/the-enemy-in-our-feeds-
e86511488de

2 https://www.amnesty.org/en/latest/news/2023/08/myanmar-
time-for-meta-to-pay-reparations-to-rohingya-for-role-in-eth-
nic-cleansing/

3 https://www.newstatesman.com/culture/books/2023/07/the-
age-of-digital-outrage

4 https://www.science.org/doi/10.1126/sciadv.abe5641

5 https://www.technologyreview.com/2021/10/05/1036519/
facebook-whistleblower-frances-haugen-algorithms/

6 Rathje, S., Van Bavel, Jay J., van der Linden, Sander, (2021),
'Out-group animosity drives engagement on social media',
Proceedings of the National Academy of Sciences (PNAS)
118(26).

7 https://www.washingtonpost.com/technology/2021/10/22/
jan-6-capitol-riot-facebook/

8 https://blog.x.com/en_us/topics/company/2020/suspension

9 https://www.theverge.com/2022/7/12/23205723/donald-trump-
twitter-tweets-january-6th-us-capitol-rally-riot-stop-the-steal

10 https://www.esafety.gov.au/newsroom/media-releases/report-re-
veals-the-extent-of-deep-cuts-to-safety-staff-and-gaps-in-twitter/
xs-measures-to-tackle-online-hate

11 https://www.globalwitness.org/en/blog/exposing-social-media-
platforms-failures-to-protect-their-users/

12 https://www.globalwitness.org/en/campaigns/digital-threats/
how-big-tech-platforms-are-neglecting-their-non-english-lan-
guage-users/

13 Ibid.

14 https://www.theverge.com/2020/5/26/21270659/facebook-division-news-feed-algorithms

15 https://www.independent.co.uk/news/uk/southport-prime-minister-english-defence-league-muslims-government-b2590217.html

16 https://integrityinstitute.org/blog/misinformation-amplification-tracking-dashboard

17 https://news.mit.edu/2018/study-twitter-false-news-travels-faster-true-stories-0308

18 Howard, Philip & Kollanyi, Bence & Bradshaw, Samantha & Neudert, Lisa-Maria. (2018). 'Social Media, News and Political Information during the US Election: Was Polarizing Content Concentrated in Swing States?'. 10.48550/arXiv.1802.03573.

19 https://www.reuters.com/investigates/special-report/myanmar-facebook-hate/

20 https://www.theguardian.com/technology/2023/dec/19/tiktok-users-including-russell-brand-given-special-status-messages-show

21 https://apnews.com/article/fact-check-starbucks-watermelon-mug-palestinians-boycott-845661004904

22 https://algorithmwatch.org/en/study-microsofts-bing-chat/

23 https://www.theguardian.com/world/2022/nov/16/iran-protests-social-media-death-penalty

24 https://qz.com/1264547/facebooks-problems-can-be-solved-with-design

25 *Woman's Hour*, BBC Radio 4, 17 January 2024. Available at: https://www.bbc.co.uk/programmes/poh5k8rl

26 Naomi Klein, *Doppelganger* (Allen Lane, 2023), p.12.

27 *Woman's Hour*, BBC Radio 4, 17 January 2024.

Chapter 7: Body Goals

1 Emma Dabiri, *Disobedient Bodies* (Wellcome Collection, 2023), pp. 18–19.

2 https://www.abc.net.au/triplej/programs/hack/facebook-whis-tleblower-says-instagram-content-hurts-teens/13573020

3 https://counterhate.com/research/deadly-by-design/

4 https://www.england.nhs.uk/2022/03/nhs-treating-record-num-ber-of-young-people-for-eating-disorders/

5 https://link.springer.com/article/10.1007/s40519-023-01550-7

6 https://counterhate.com/research/tiktoks-toxic-trade/

7 https://www.sciencedirect.com/science/article/abs/pii/S1740144519305753

8 https://news.sky.com/story/facebook-whistleblower-live-franc-es-haugen-appears-before-uk-parliamentary-commit-tee-12444217

9 Marika Tiggemann, Isabella Anderberg, Zoe Brown, 'Upload-ing your best self: Selfie editing and body dissatisfaction', *Body Image*, Vol. 33, 2020, 175-182. https://doi.org/10.1016/j.bodyim.2020.03.002.

10 https://pubmed.ncbi.nlm.nih.gov/28251592/

11 https://www.abc.net.au/triplej/programs/hack/facebook-whis-tleblower-says-instagram-content-hurts-teens/13573020

12 Mary McGill, *The Visibility Trap* (New Island Books, 2021), p.64

13 https://www.dazeddigital.com/beauty/article/60860/1/we-were-never-supposed-to-see-our-faces-this-much-social-media-zoom

14 Hoffman, Claire (15 September 2010). 'The Battle for Facebook'. *Rolling Stone*. Wenner Media. Archived from the original on 26 December 2018. Retrieved 24 June 2017.

15 https://www.theguardian.com/technology/2023/feb/08/biased-ai-algorithms-racy-women-bodies

16 https://algorithmwatch.org/en/instagram-algorithm-nudity/

17 *Disobedient Bodies*, p.19.

18 https://www.dailymail.co.uk/femail/article-9291463/Harley-Street-doctor-reveals-five-faces-modern-beauty.html

19 https://twitter.com/jessf_white/status/1580183697785225216

20 https://www.forbes.com/sites/anniebrown/2021/10/27/under-standing-the-technical-and-societal-relationship-between-shad-owbanning-and-algorithmic-bias/

21 https://www.theguardian.com/technology/2020/oct/20/instagram-censored-one-of-these-photos-but-not-the-other-we-must-ask-why

22 https://www.uswitch.com/mobiles/studies/mobile-statistics/

23 https://committees.parliament.uk/writtenevidence/42858/pdf/

24 https://www.transform-our-world.org/files/values_to_trans-form_our_world_white_paper.pdf

25 https://amp-theguardian-com.cdn.ampproject.org/c/s/amp.theguardian.com/society/2023/sep/13/happiness-of-girls-and-young-women-at-lowest-level-since-2009-shows-uk-poll

26 https://www.glamourmagazine.co.uk/article/enhanced-photos-social-media-law

27 https://www.vogue.co.uk/article/summer-body

Chapter 8: Misogyny's Newer Model

1 https://foreignpolicy.com/2017/01/16/women-vs-the-machine/

2 https://refuge.org.uk/wp-content/uploads/2022/11/Marked-as-Unsafe-report-FINAL.pdf

3 Gerd Gigerenzer, *How to Stay Smart in a Smart World* (Allen Lane, 2022), p.177

4 https://www.channel4.com/news/nearly-19000-victims-of-so-called-revenge-porn-in-four-years-investigation-finds-2

5 https://www.nbcnews.com/tech/social-media/inside-facebook-s-efforts-stop-revenge-porn-it-spreads-n1083631

6 https://www.mirror.co.uk/news/uk-news/campaigners-fury-on-ly-3-revenge-28305159

7 https://inews.co.uk/inews-lifestyle/deep-fake-porn-fabricated-videos-harm-women-1879934

8 https://www.thetimes.com/uk/law/article/georgia-harrison-in-terview-revenge-porn-g6pc978bx

9 https://www.kcl.ac.uk/news/masculinity-and-womens-equali-ty-study-finds-emerging-gender-divide-in-young-peoples-atti-tudes

10 https://www.reddit.com/r/Teachers/comments/wqvn9a/the_rise_of_andrew_tate_is_ruining_my_freshman/

11 https://www.amnesty.org.uk/press-releases/women-abused-twitter-every-30-seconds-new-study

12 https://audri.org/new-research-brief-doxing-digital-abuse-and-the-law/

13 https://www.independent.co.uk/voices/commentators/laurie-penny-a-woman-s-opinion-is-the-miniskirt-of-the-inter-net-6256946.html

14 https://cdt.org/insights/an-unrepresentative-democra-cy-how-disinformation-and-online-abuse-hinder-wom-en-of-color-political-candidates-in-the-united-states/

15 https://www.amnesty.org.uk/online-violence-women-mps

16 https://news.sky.com/story/a-day-out-with-labour-mp-zarah-sultana-reveals-how-she-constantly-has-to-think-about-her-safety-13093690

17 https://equalitynow.org/news_and_insights/new-research-brief-doxing-digital-abuse-and-the-law/

18 https://www.bbc.co.uk/news/technology-62908601

19 https://www.theguardian.com/society/2022/oct/30/global-in-cel-culture-terrorism-misogyny-violent-action-forums

20 https://macleans.ca/longforms/incel-terrorism/

21 https://www.washingtonpost.com/technology/2022/09/22/incels-rape-murder-study/

22 https://www.poolre.co.uk/terrorism-threat-publications/andrew-tate-admirer-jailed-following-university-attack-plot/

23 https://www.bbc.co.uk/news/articles/cne4vw1x83po

24 https://www.counterterrorism.police.uk/new-prevent-statistics-warn-of-increase-in-young-men-becoming-fixated-on-violent-extremism/

25 https://www.vodafone.co.uk/newscentre/press-release/ai-aggro-rithms/

26 https://www.adl.org/blog/online-poll-results-provide-new-insights-into-incel-community

27 https://www.qualitativecriminology.com/pub/z1961qto/release/1

28 https://www.nytimes.com/interactive/2021/12/09/us/where-the-despairing-log-on.html

29 https://counterhate.com/research/incelosphere/

30 https://bdnews24.com/socialmedia/where-the-despairing-log-on-and-learn-ways-to-die

31 https://journals.sagepub.com/doi/10.1177/10778012231222486

Chapter 9: Workers, Not Robots

1 Phil Jones, *Work Without the Worker* (Verso, 2021), p.6

2 https://www.ringover.com/blog/loneliness-at-work-survey

3 https://www.huckmag.com/article/speaking-to-amazon-uk-workers-on-the-picket-lines-in-coventry-2023

4 https://www.ifow.org/publications/what-impact-does-exposure-to-workplace-technologies-have-on-workers-quality-of-life-briefing-paper

5 https://www.tuc.org.uk/news/intrusive-worker-surveil-lance-tech-risks-spiralling-out-control-without-stronger-regula-tion

6 https://www.theguardian.com/global-development/2023/mar/26/dystopian-surveillance-disproportionately-tar-gets-young-female-minority-workers-ippr-report

7 https://iwgb.org.uk/en/post/racist-facial-recognition/

8 https://www.theguardian.com/uk-news/2024/jan/11/what-is-uk-post-office-horizon-it-scandal-about-who-involved

ENDNOTES

9   https://www.tuc.org.uk/news/gig-economy-workforce-england-and-wales-has-almost-tripled-last-five-years-new-tuc-research
10 https://novaramedia.com/2021/12/14/with-uber-paying-them-peanuts-exploited-drivers-are-cancelling-rides/
11 https://www.tuc.org.uk/research-analysis/reports/ai-bill-project
12 https://www.businessinsider.com/meet-uber-drivers-won-five-years-legal-fight-worker-rights-2021-2
13 https://www.theguardian.com/technology/2023/jul/12/former-uber-driver-wins-payout-of-20000-owed-for-more-than-seve-years
14 https://fair.work/en/fw/impact/
15 https://news.sky.com/story/meta-is-planning-to-use-your-face-book-and-instagram-posts-to-train-ai-and-not-everyone-can-opt-out-13158655
16 https://arstechnica.com/tech-policy/2023/04/stable-diffusion-copyright-lawsuits-could-be-a-legal-earthquake-for-ai/
17 https://www.techtarget.com/searchenterpriseai/news/366544611/A-look-at-writers-battle-to-get-AI-vendors-to-pay-them
18 https://www.huckmag.com/article/the-digital-artists-fighting-back-against-ai
19 https://www.theguardian.com/culture/2023/oct/01/holly-wood-writers-strike-artificial-intelligence
20 https://autonomy.work/portfolio/gpt-4-day-week-gb-edition/

Chapter 10: I Post, Therefore I Am

1   Lauren Oyler, *Fake Accounts* (4th Estate, 2021), p.69
2   'Jia Tolentino on the Internet's Endless Stage', *Offline with Jon Favreau*, 24 October 2021. Available at: https://open.spotify.com/episode/3tyltsXo5040qwfMPtI3cu?si=6713d0b559eb4e1e
3   Jenny Odell, *How to Do Nothing*, (Melville House, 2019), p.15
4   'Influencers with Taylor Lorenz', *You're Wrong About*, 12 December 2023. Available at: https://open.spotify.com/episode/5Zh-WOfzsfERKXzpHSRPBWg?si=yYFB5YUPSF61GOKfQno5pw

270

5   https://www.dazeddigital.com/life-culture/article/61845/1/we-doc-ument-our-whole-lives-online-but-is-it-even-worth-it-anymore

6   *How To Do Nothing*, p.1

7   https://www.agilitypr.com/pr-news/public-relations/influencer-inhibitors-4-out-of-5-of-content-creators-are-burnt-out-strug-gle-with-mental-health/

8   https://www.businessinsider.com/youtuber-jordi-van-den-bussche-interview-ai-replacement-burnout-2023-8

9   Anthony Elliott, *Algorithmic Intimacy* (Polity, 2022), p.12.

10 'What's Your Algorithm?', *The Sound Bath*, 5 May 2022. Available at: https://open.spotify.com/episode/2t2pMlskonAY-HxVeGg1Fdf?si=70c00c09d7e64ca5

11 https://news.gallup.com/opinion/gallup/512618/almost-quarter-world-feels-lonely.aspx

Chapter 11: Keep Up or Carry On

1   https://x.com/ilanaslightly/status/1617223745437069314

2   https://www.lloydsbank.com/assets/media/pdfs/bank-ing_with_us/whats-happening/221103-lloyds-consumer-digi-tal-index-2022-report.pdf

3   https://publications.parliament.uk/pa/ld5803/ldselect/ldcomm/219/219.pdf

4   https://www.bbc.co.uk/news/uk-66130785

5   https://www.independentage.org/news-media/press-releases/new-data-shows-online-scams-cost-older-people-an-average-of-ps4000-but

6   https://www.theguardian.com/money/2022/jun/29/uk-victims-lost-13bn-in-2021-amid-surge-in-online-new-data-shows

7   https://www.gov.uk/government/publications/essential-dig-ital-skills-framework/essential-digital-skills-framework#be-ing-safe-and-legal-online

8   https://www.greatermanchester-ca.gov.uk/what-we-do/digital/
    digital-inclusion-agenda/
9   https://www.theguardian.com/technology/2021/may/10/
    smartphone-is-now-the-place-where-we-live-anthropologists-say
10 https://www.goodthingsfoundation.org/insights/digital-exclu-
    sion-and-health-inequalities/
11 https://www.gponline.com/four-five-doctors-fear-in-
    creased-remote-consultations-impact-vulnerable-survey-finds/
    article/1702829
12 Meredith Broussard, *More Than a Glitch* (MIT Press, 2023),
    p.92
13 https://www.ageuk.org.uk/london/about-us/news/articles/2023/
    access-denied/
14 https://www.ons.gov.uk/peoplepopulationandcommunity/
    householdcharacteristics/homeinternetandsocialmediausage/
    articles/exploringtheuksdigitaldivide/2019-03-04
15 https://committees.parliament.uk/writtenevidence/123155/html/
16 https://www.thetimes.com/article/2000-job-cuts-train-ticket-of-
    fices-uk-consultation-closures-tltbg0qz6
17 https://tribunemag.co.uk/2023/07/i-dont-know-how-ill-cope-if-
    they-disappear-the-fight-to-save-ticket-offices
18 https://x.com/petepaphides/status/1528735492052762624
19 https://www.euronews.com/next/2022/02/22/i-m-old-not-
    stupid-campaigning-pensioner-forces-spanish-banks-to-tackle-
    exclusion-of-elder

Conclusion: Ctrl + Alt + Reclaim

1   Cory Doctorow, *The Internet Con* (Verso, 2023), p.18.
2   https://mentalhellth.xyz/p/horrible-airplane-seat-with-hd-tele-
    vision

Credits

Trapeze would like to thank everyone at Orion who worked on the publication of *Logging Off*.

Agent
Megan Staunton

Editor
Katie Ogunsakin

Copy-editor
Ian Greensill

Proofreader
Clare Wallis

Editorial Management
Sarah Fortune
Pablo Pizarro Janczur
Jane Hughes
Charlie Panayiotou
Lucy Bilton
Patrice Nelson

Audio
Paul Stark
Louise Richardson
Georgina Cutler-Ross

Contracts
Rachel Monte
Ellie Bowker
Tabitha Gresty

Design
Jessica Hart
Nick Shah
Deborah Francois
Helen Ewing

Photo Shoots & Image Research
Natalie Dawkins

Finance
Nick Gibson
Jasdip Nandra
Sue Baker
Tom Costello

Inventory
Jo Jacobs
Dan Stevens

Production
Hannah Cox
Katie Horrocks

Marketing
Louis Patel

Publicity
Sarah Lundy

Sales
Dave Murphy
Victoria Laws
Esther Waters
Group Sales teams across
Digital, Field, Inter-
national and Non-Trade

Operations
Group Sales Operations
team

Rights
Rebecca Folland
Tara Hiatt
Ben Fowler
Maddie Stephens
Ruth Blakemore
Marie Henckel

About the Author

Adele Zeynep Walton is a British Turkish journalist and online safety campaigner.

Adele has channelled a personal loss into advocating for a safer digital world for young people. She is a member of Bereaved Families for Online Safety and a youth ambassador for People Vs Big Tech.

As a freelance journalist Adele has written for the *Independent, Dazed, i-D, VICE, Metro, The Big Issue* and more. Her articles have been translated into several languages and she has been featured on LBC, Sky News, BBC Radio Scotland and Channel 4 News. Between 2023–2024, Adele was *Dazed*'s first ever political book columnist, where she interviewed authors including Naomi Klein, Emma Dabiri and Vicky Spratt.

She is also the co-founder of Logging Off Club, which brings people together offline at phone-free events to reconnect and promote connection, curiosity and wellness.

Adele was the recipient of a Society of Authors' Foundation grant (2023) and this is her first book.